I0820844

Early
SPACE
Encyclopedias

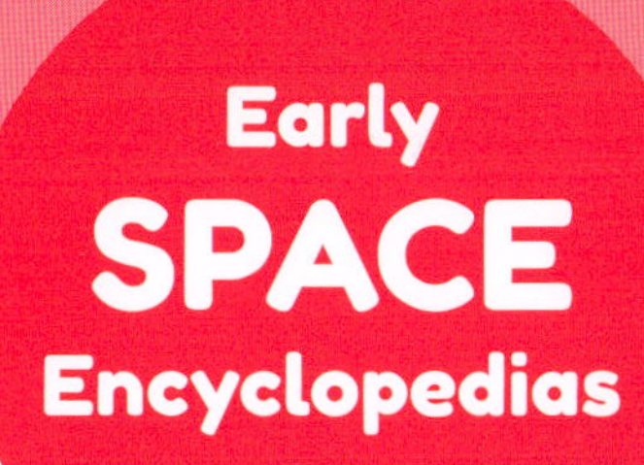

THE MOON

by Sue Bradford Edwards

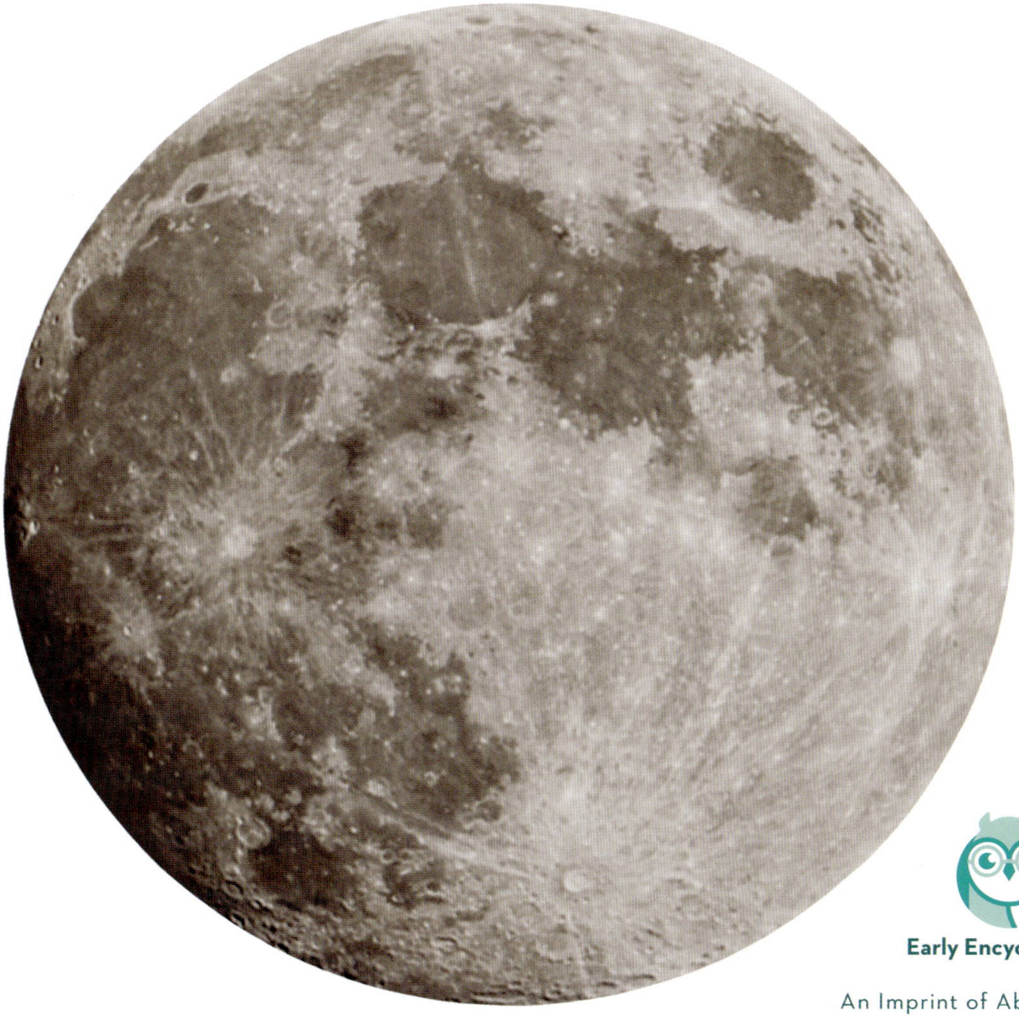

Early Encyclopedias

An Imprint of Abdo Reference
abdobooks.com

abdobooks.com

Published by Abdo Reference, a division of ABDO, PO Box 398166, Minneapolis, Minnesota 55439.

Printed in China.
102025
012026

Editor: Arnold Ringstad
Series Designers: Candice Keimig, Joshua Olson
Production Designer: Ryan Gale

Library of Congress Control Number: 2025939292

Publisher's Cataloging-in-Publication Data

Names: Edwards, Sue Bradford, author.
Title: The moon / by Sue Bradford Edwards
Description: Minneapolis, Minnesota: Abdo Reference, 2026 | Series: Early space encyclopedias | Includes online resources and index.
Identifiers: ISBN 9781098298784 (lib. bdg.) | ISBN 9798384932581 (ebook)
Subjects: LCSH: Outer space--Exploration--Juvenile literature. | Astronomy--Juvenile literature. | Solar System--Juvenile literature. | Moon--Juvenile literature. | Sky--Juvenile literature. | Encyclopedias--Juvenile literature.
Classification: DDC 523.3--dc23

CONTENTS

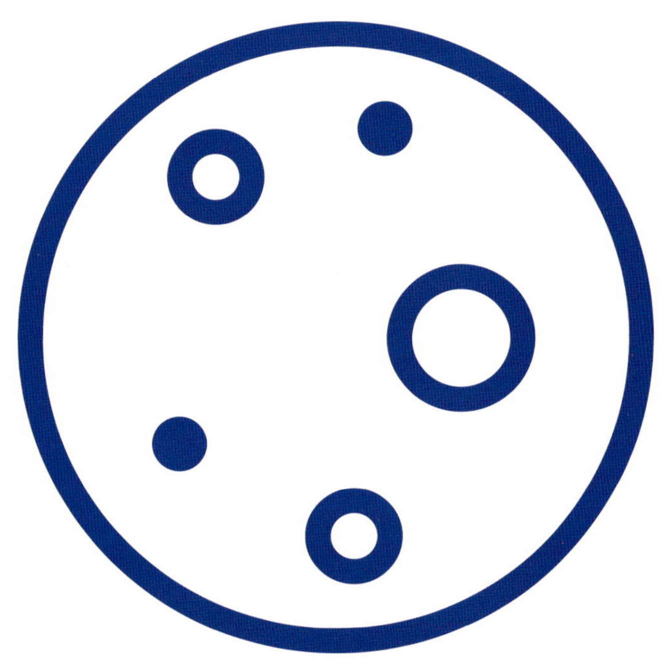

Human-Made Satellites

People launch satellites into space. These satellites do many jobs. Some help track the weather. Others carry data for phones and computers.

A Satellite

A satellite is an object that orbits a larger object in space. The moon is Earth's only natural satellite. Earth's other satellites are made by people. Rockets launch these satellites into orbit.

The moon is much closer to Earth than the other planets are.

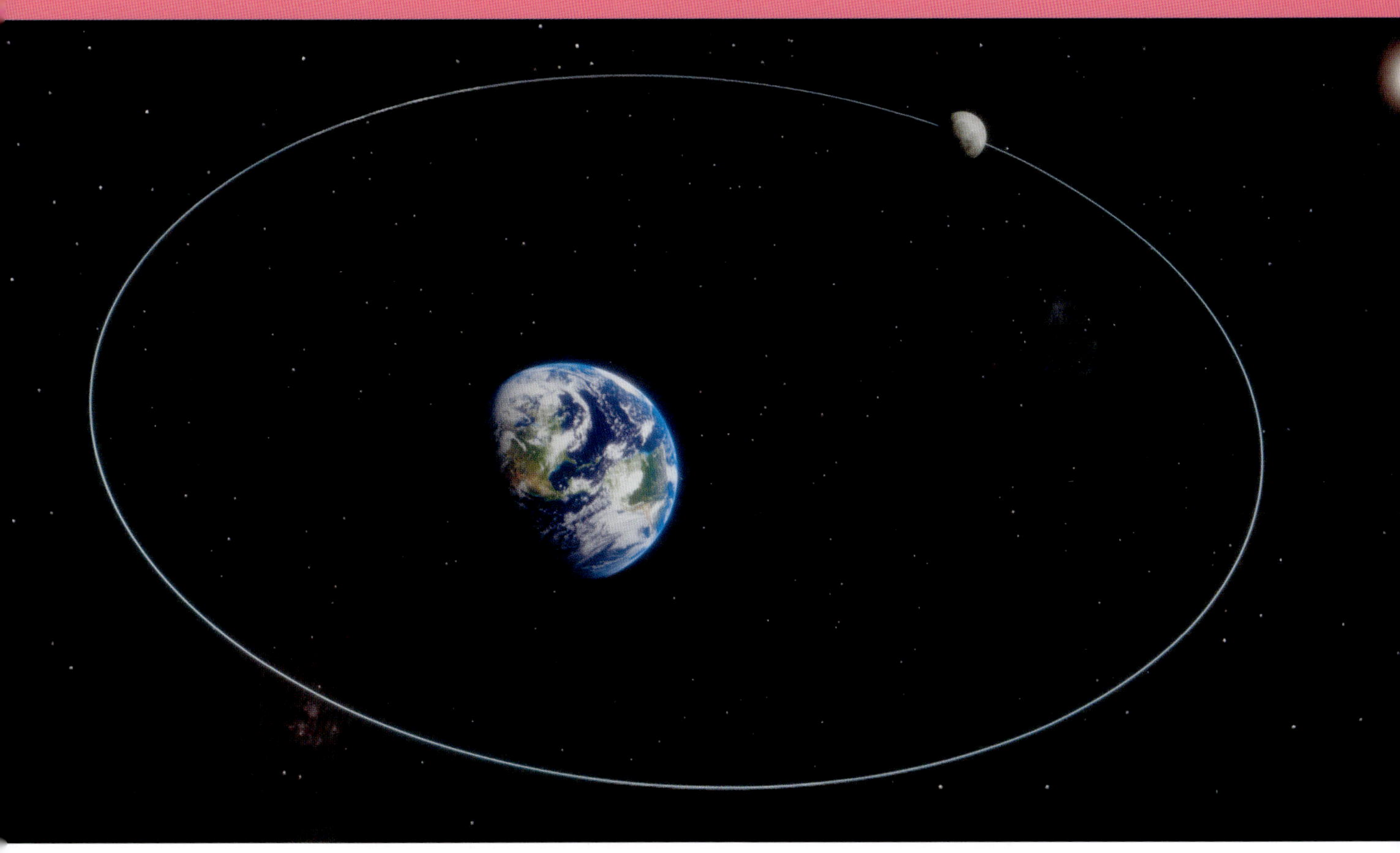

The moon's distance from Earth changes during its orbit.

Distance

The moon's orbit is not perfectly round. It is an oval. This means the moon's distance from Earth varies. Sometimes it is closer. Other times it is farther away. On average, the moon is 238,855 miles (384,400 km) from Earth.

The Moon's Name

Early European scientists studied the moon. They wrote about it in Latin. In this language, the moon is called Luna. The word *lunar* is still used for things related to the moon. Rocks from the moon are lunar rocks.

Size

The solar system includes the sun and all the objects around it. Earth's moon is one of the solar system's largest moons. It is about 2,160 miles (3,476 km) across. That makes it about one-fourth the width of Earth.

Studying the Moon

The moon is large in the night sky. People have studied it since ancient times. Telescopes helped reveal more details. Later, spacecraft studied the moon up close. Scientists tried to figure out how it formed.

Ptolemy was an ancient Greek scientist who studied the moon.

The early moon, *right*, may have been thrown apart from the material that formed Earth.

Theories

One theory was that the moon was once part of Earth. Long ago, Earth spun more quickly. Material was thrown off the planet. This material gathered together. It became the moon. Another theory was that the moon started as an asteroid. It passed close to Earth. The planet's gravity captured it.

A huge impact in the distant past probably created the moon.

Impact

Scientists now think one theory is the most likely. The young Earth was struck by a smaller planet. The impact threw material into space. Over time, gravity pulled this material together. It formed the moon.

Evidence

There is good evidence for this theory. Scientists studied lunar rocks. These are very similar to Earth rocks. This suggests Earth and the moon are made from the same material.

Samples from the moon provided more evidence for the impact theory.

Aristotle

In 300 BCE, the Greek thinker Aristotle studied the moon. He thought it looked like a smooth, round ball. Aristotle saw dark patches on the moon. He thought Earth had stained it.

Besides astronomy, Aristotle also studied biology, politics, art, and more.

The First Telescopes

In the early 1600s, scientists invented telescopes. These devices made distant things look closer. Scientists could see the moon in greater detail.

Galileo made many discoveries about the moon and other objects in space.

Galileo's Observations

The Italian thinker Galileo Galilei studied the night sky. He looked at the moon through his telescope. It made things look eight times larger.

Galileo's Telescope

Galileo's telescope was a simple tube with two lenses. They were fixed in place. The focus could not be changed.

Galileo saw gray patches and changing shadows. He understood he was seeing mountains and pits. The moon was not smooth. He drew what he saw.

Galileo's Findings

Galileo published his findings in 1610. He called this work *Sidereus Nuncius*. This title means "starry messenger." Other scientists argued about his findings. But they came to accept his work over time.

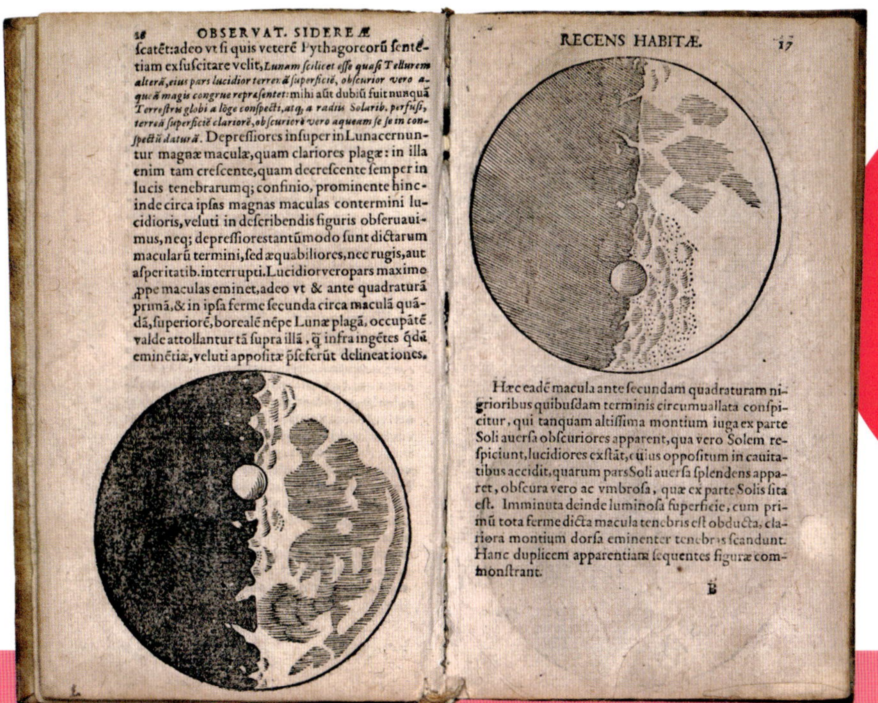

18 OBSERVAT. SIDEREÆ

ſcatēt:adeo vt ſi quis veterē Pythagoreorū ſentētiam exſuſcitare velit, *Lunam ſcilicet eſſe quaſi Tellurem alterā, eius pars lucidior terrenā ſuperficiē, obſcurior vero aqueā magis congrue repræſentet:* mihi aūt dubiū fuit nunquā *Terreſtris globi a lōge conſpecti, atq; a radiis Solarib. perfuſi, terreā ſuperficiē clariorē, obſcuriorē vero aqueam ſe ſe in conſpectū daturā.* Depreſſiores inſuper in Luna cernuntur magnæ maculæ, quam clariores plagæ: in illa enim tam creſcente, quam decreſcente ſemper in lucis tenebrarumq; confinio, prominente hincinde circa ipſas magnas maculas contermini lucidioris, veluti in deſcribendis figuris obſeruauimus, neq; depreſſiores tantūmodo ſunt dictarum macularū termini, ſed æquabiliores, nec rugis, aut aſperitatib. interrupti. Lucidior vero pars maxime ppe maculas eminet, adeo vt & ante quadraturā primā, & in ipſa ferme ſecunda circa maculā quādā, ſuperiorē, borealē nēpe Lunæ plagā, occupātē valde attollantur tā ſupra illā, q̃ infra ingētes q̄dā eminētiæ, veluti appoſitæ pſeferūt delineationes.

RECENS HABITÆ. 17

Hæc eadē macula ante ſecundam quadraturam nigrioribus quibuſdam terminis circumuallata conſpicitur, qui tanquam altiſſima montium iuga ex parte Soli auerſa obſcuriores apparent, qua vero Solem reſpiciunt, lucidiores exſtāt, cuius oppoſitum in cauitatibus accidit, quarum pars Soli auerſa ſplendens apparet, obſcura vero ac vmbroſa, quæ ex parte Solis ſita eſt. Imminuta deinde luminoſa ſuperficie, cum primū tota ferme dicta macula tenebris eſt obducta, clariora montium dorſa eminenter tenebras ſcandunt. Hanc duplicem apparentiam ſequentes figuræ commonſtrant.

B

Galileo's work improved the scientific understanding of the moon.

Sea and Land

After Galileo's work, people thought the moon was like Earth. They called the darker areas *maria*. This is the Latin word for "seas." They called the lighter areas *terrae*. This is Latin for "lands."

The maria are the moon's dark, flat plains.

Strange, false stories about life on the moon spread in the 1800s.

Life on the Moon?

People wondered if the moon might have life. In 1835, the *New York Sun* printed articles about this. The articles claimed there were goats on the moon. Articles told stories of unicorns and people with bat wings. But readers soon learned the stories were made up.

Scientists built large telescopes in the 1800s.

Learning More

In the 1800s, telescopes improved. Scientists learned more about objects in space. They came up with new theories. Some scientists thought volcanoes created the moon's craters. Others believed meteorite impacts made the craters.

Not Earth-Like

Telescopes got even better in the 1900s. People saw the moon more clearly. They saw that it did not look like Earth. The moon seemed unlikely to have Earth-like plants or animals. But some people still thought it might have simple life. It was hard to know for sure without going there.

In the 1930s, an observatory in California created a huge map of the moon based on its telescope studies.

The Space Race

In 1957, the Soviet Union launched the first human-made satellite. It was called *Sputnik 1*. The United States soon launched its own satellite. The two countries competed in space technology. This included sending spacecraft to the moon.

A Soviet museum showed a life-size copy of *Sputnik 1*.

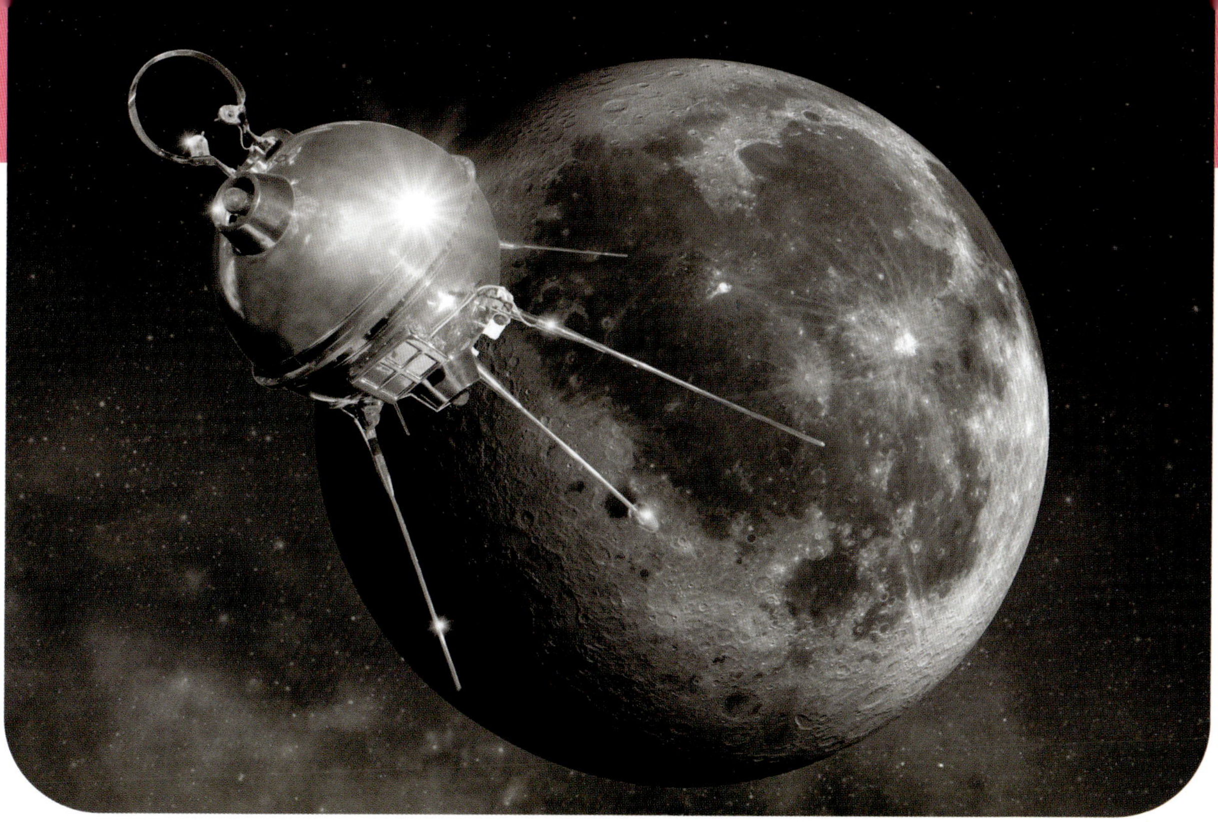

Luna 1 passed about 3,700 miles (6,000 km) from the moon.

The First Moon Missions

The Soviet Union launched *Luna 1* in January 1959. It was the first spacecraft to leave Earth orbit. It was designed to crash into the moon. But it missed. It was still the first probe to pass near the moon.

FUN FACT!

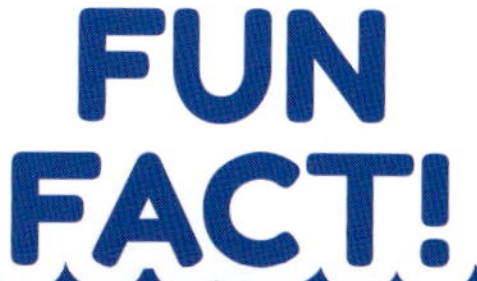

The US *Pioneer 4* spacecraft flew past the moon in March 1959.

Yuri Gagarin launched aboard a Vostok-K rocket.

People in Space

Human spaceflight was also advancing. Yuri Gagarin became the first person in space. The Soviet Union launched him into orbit in April 1961. US astronauts followed. Both nations worked to build better spacecraft. This would be needed for a long journey to the moon.

Kennedy's Challenge

US president John F. Kennedy gave a speech in May 1961. He supported the National Aeronautics and Space Administration (NASA). This is the US space agency responsible for space exploration. Kennedy challenged the nation to land astronauts on the moon by the end of the 1960s.

Ranger Program

The US Ranger program sent more probes to explore the moon. The program ran from 1961 to 1965. Probes took photos of the moon. They helped NASA prepare for future landings.

Workers prepared *Ranger 7* for launch in 1963.

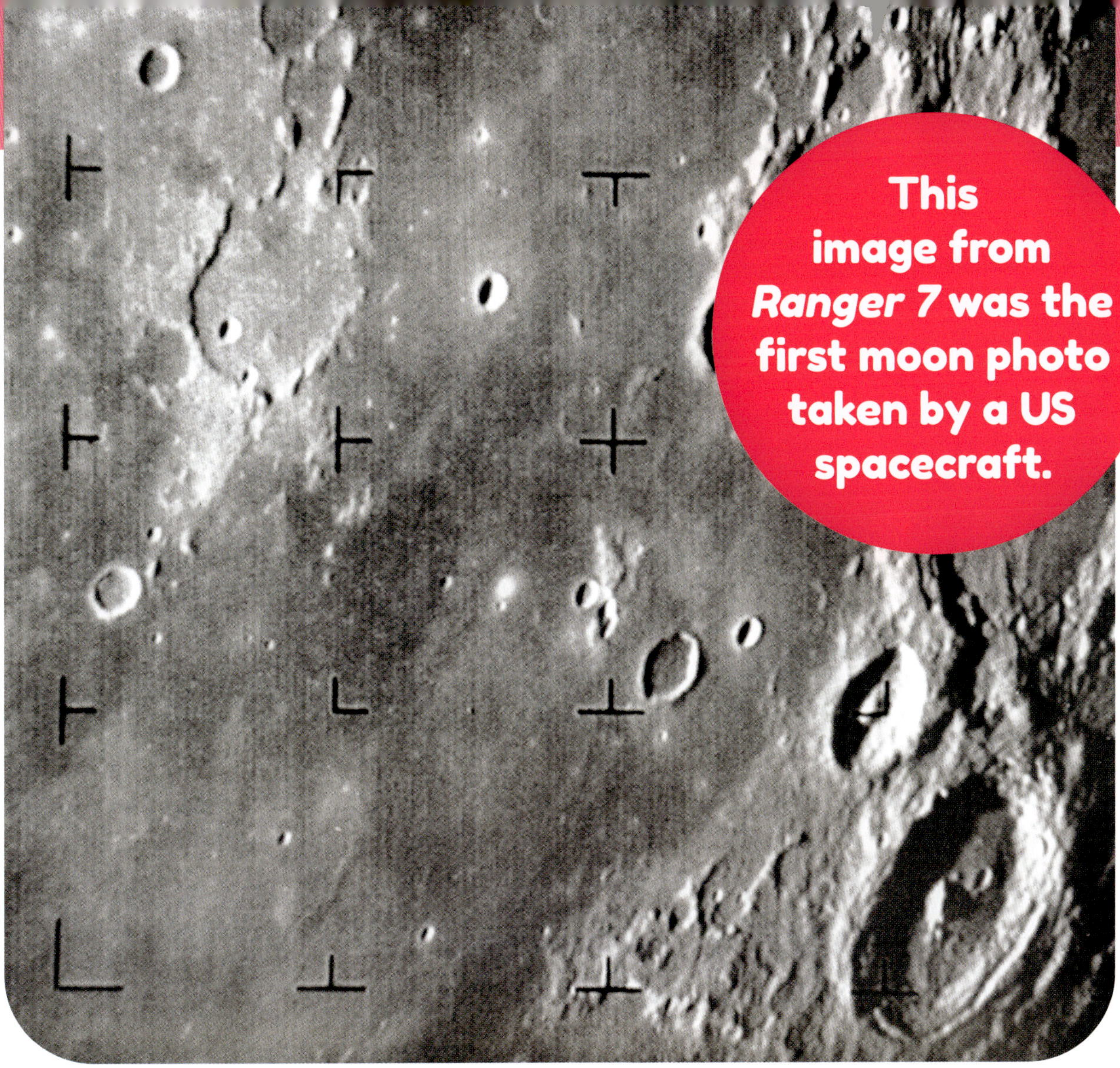

This image from *Ranger 7* was the first moon photo taken by a US spacecraft.

Close-Up Photos

Rangers 7, 8, and *9* were successful. The probes were aimed directly at the moon. They took pictures up until impact. The photos were clear and detailed.

FUN FACT!

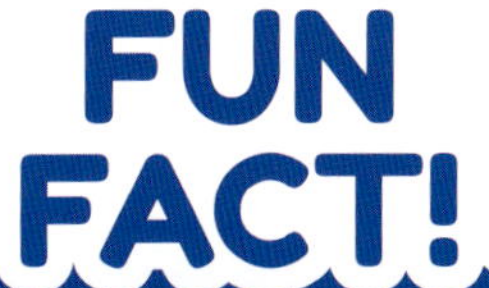

Ranger 8 sent back more than 7,100 images before crashing.

***Luna 9*'s shell unfolded after landing to keep the spacecraft stable.**

Luna Program

The Soviet Union sent more lunar probes too. *Luna 9* was the first spacecraft to land on the moon. It touched down in February 1966. The lander sent back pictures and other data.

FUN FACT!

Operators back on Earth drove *Lunokhod 1* by remote control.

Samples and Rovers

Luna 16 landed on the moon in September 1970. It collected lunar soil. Then it launched the sample back to Earth in a small rocket. *Luna 17* landed with a robotic rover called *Lunokhod 1* in November 1970. The rover drove several miles. It studied soil and took photos.

The *Lunokhod 1* rover was powered by a solar panel.

Surveyor

The United States also sent robotic landers. These were part of the Surveyor program. Five probes landed between 1966 and 1968. NASA practiced landing on the moon. It also studied future human landing sites.

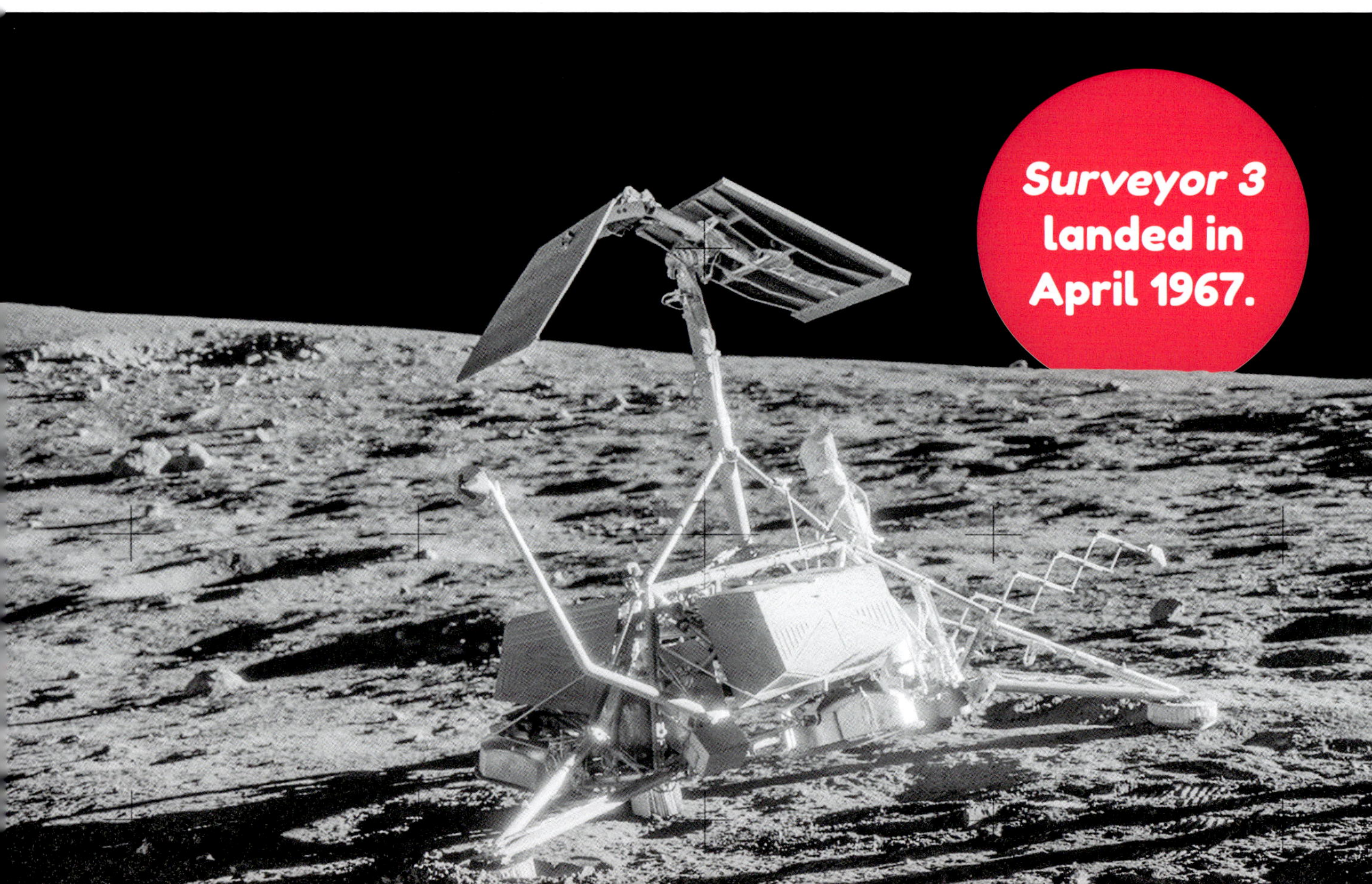

Surveyor 3 **landed in April 1967.**

The Lunar Orbiter probes took photos and then beamed them back to Earth.

Lunar Orbiter

Another US program sent spacecraft to orbit the moon. Five Lunar Orbiter probes flew to the moon in 1966 and 1967. They mapped the surface in high detail. This helped NASA plan its human landings.

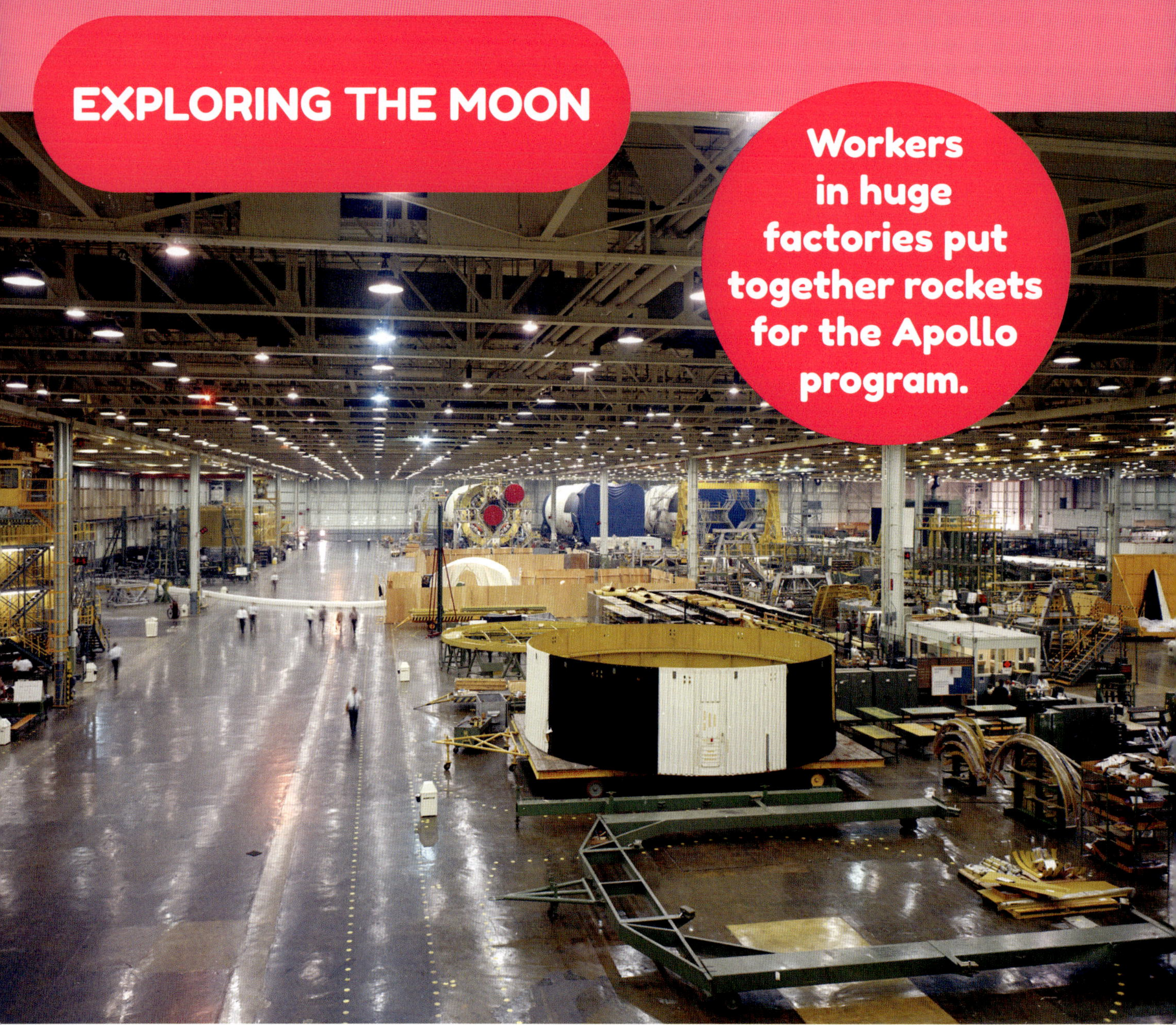

Workers in huge factories put together rockets for the Apollo program.

Apollo Program

The project to meet Kennedy's goal was the Apollo program. This effort took a huge amount of work. Thousands of people played a part.

Rockets and Spacecraft

NASA used the powerful Saturn V rocket for Apollo. Astronauts would ride in the cone-shaped command module. They would land the spider-like lunar module on the moon.

Workers check a lunar module before launch.

Space Suit

The astronauts would not simply land on the moon. They would also get out of the spacecraft and walk around. They needed new space suits for this. Workers spent years designing and testing a space suit for moon walking.

Astronauts practiced working in their space suits on Earth.

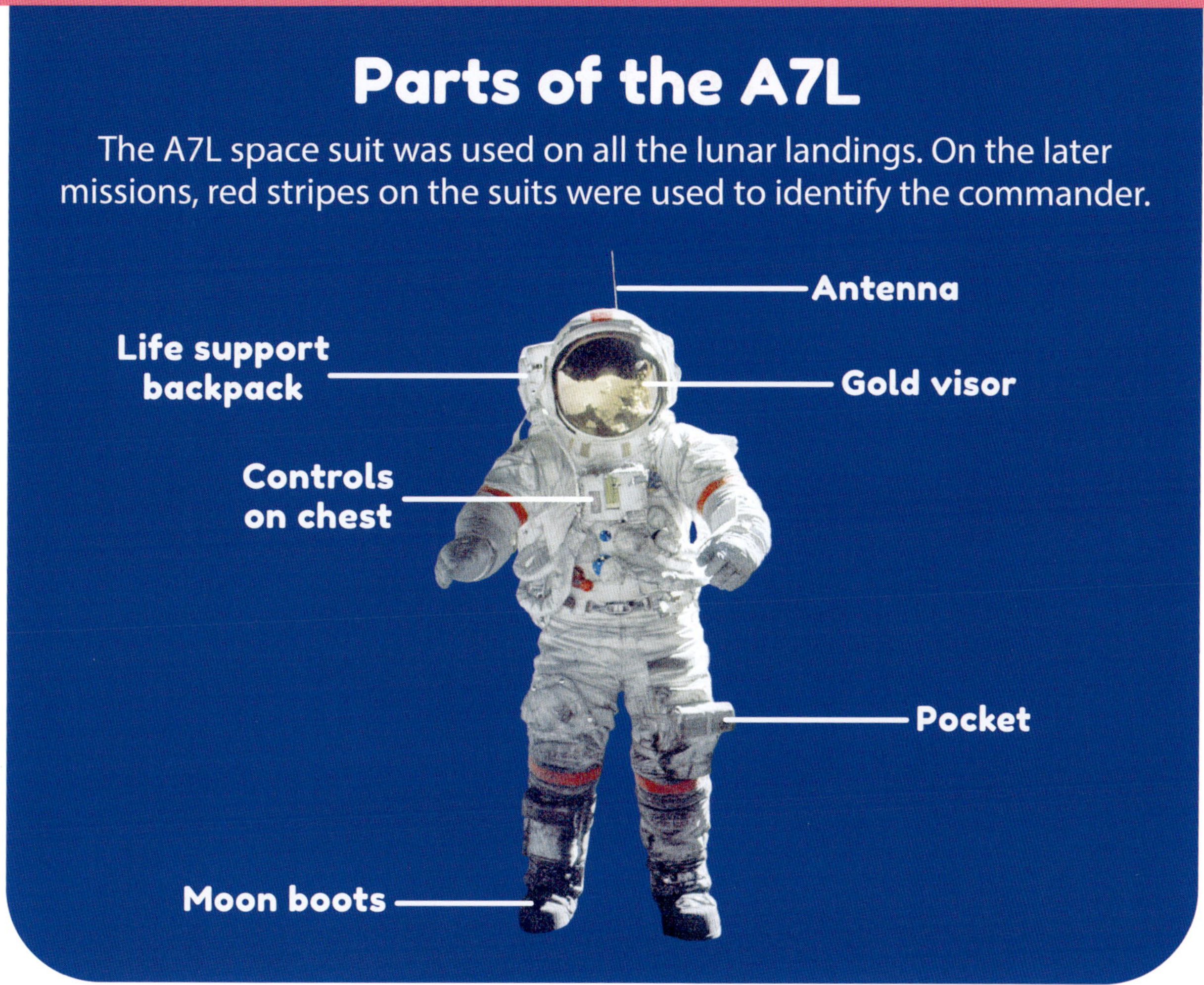

The A7L

The Apollo space suit was called the A7L. It was like a personal spacecraft for each astronaut. The suit provided air to breathe. It kept the astronaut at a safe temperature. Radios in the suit let astronauts talk to each other.

Apollo 8 astronaut Bill Anders took a famous photo called *Earthrise*.

Early Apollo Missions

The first Apollo mission to launch was Apollo 7. Astronauts tested the command module in Earth orbit. Apollo 8 flew around the moon. But it did not bring a lander. The astronauts tested the command module in lunar orbit.

Preparing for the Moon

Apollo 9 included a lunar module. Astronauts tested it in Earth orbit. Apollo 10 brought a lunar module to the moon. The astronauts separated it from the command module. They got within a few miles of the lunar surface. Then they returned home. NASA had now tested everything but the landing. That would be the next mission's goal.

Apollo 9 astronaut David Scott went on a space walk in Earth orbit.

Reflectors

The Apollo 11 astronauts left a reflector on the moon. Scientists on Earth can fire lasers at the reflector. This lets them figure out the distance between Earth and the moon.

Apollo 11

Apollo 11 launched on July 16, 1969. On July 20, the lunar module touched down. Neil Armstrong and Buzz Aldrin walked on the moon's surface. Michael Collins waited in lunar orbit.

The lunar module used a powerful rocket engine to slow down for landing.

Armstrong held the camera, so almost all of the photos from the Apollo 11 landing show Aldrin.

Walking on the Moon

Armstrong and Aldrin spent about 2 hours and 30 minutes outside. The astronauts set up science experiments. They took many photos. They also collected rocks and soil. Then they returned to the lander. They launched to rejoin Collins in orbit. The three astronauts returned home safely.

Touching down near a Surveyor probe showed that astronauts could make targeted landings on the moon.

Apollo 12

Apollo 12 landed on the moon in November 1969. The astronauts touched down near one of the Surveyor probes. They brought a piece of it back to Earth.

Apollo 13

The Apollo 13 mission launched in April 1970. But there was an explosion in the spacecraft. NASA canceled the moon landing. The astronauts worked to survive and return home. After a dangerous journey, they landed safely on Earth.

Apollo 14

Apollo 14 was the next landing. It touched down in February 1971. The crew explored an area called the Fra Mauro highlands. The astronauts gathered more samples. Some rocks came from a nearby crater.

Alan Shepard, the first American in space, commanded the Apollo 14 mission.

Later Landings

Apollos 15 and 16 were more advanced missions. Astronauts could stay on the surface longer. They also brought lunar roving vehicles. These small cars let the astronauts cover more ground. The astronauts gathered samples and scientific data.

The lunar roving vehicles opened up new possibilities for lunar exploration.

Harrison Schmitt took this photo of Eugene Cernan in the lunar module after Apollo 17's final moon walk.

The Last Landing

Apollo 17 was the final landing. Astronauts Eugene Cernan and Harrison Schmitt walked on the moon. On December 14, 1972, the astronauts took their last steps on the moon. By 2025, no humans had returned there.

First Scientist

Harrison Schmitt was a geologist. He was the first scientist on the moon. All the other moon walkers were pilots.

Thousands of *Clementine* images were combined to create this image of the moon's far side.

Clementine

Clementine was a robotic spacecraft. It launched in January 1994. For two months, it orbited the moon. It took photos to create new maps. The moon maps were the most detailed ever made. *Clementine* also found signs of water in some craters.

Lunar Prospector

Lunar Prospector was another orbiting probe. It arrived at the moon in January 1998. The probe orbited 62 miles (100 km) above the moon. It studied the lunar soil from orbit.

An artist's image shows *Lunar Prospector* during its mission.

Lunar Reconnaissance Orbiter (LRO)

The *Lunar Reconnaissance Orbiter* (*LRO*) launched in June 2009. It took the best photos yet of the moon. Scientists used these to create new maps. They searched for good places for future landings.

FUN FACT!

LRO **was still active in 2025, more than 16 years after launch.**

Workers test the *LRO* spacecraft ahead of launch.

The Apollo 17 lunar module is at the center of this *LRO* photo.

Seeing Apollo

The *LRO* photos are amazingly sharp. The Apollo landing sites can be seen. The images show the part of the lunar module left behind. The lunar rovers are visible. Even the astronauts' footsteps can be seen.

Viewing Tycho

- In June 2011, *LRO* took a photo of a lunar mountain.
- The mountain sits in the middle of the crater Tycho. This huge crater is clearly visible on the side of the moon facing Earth.

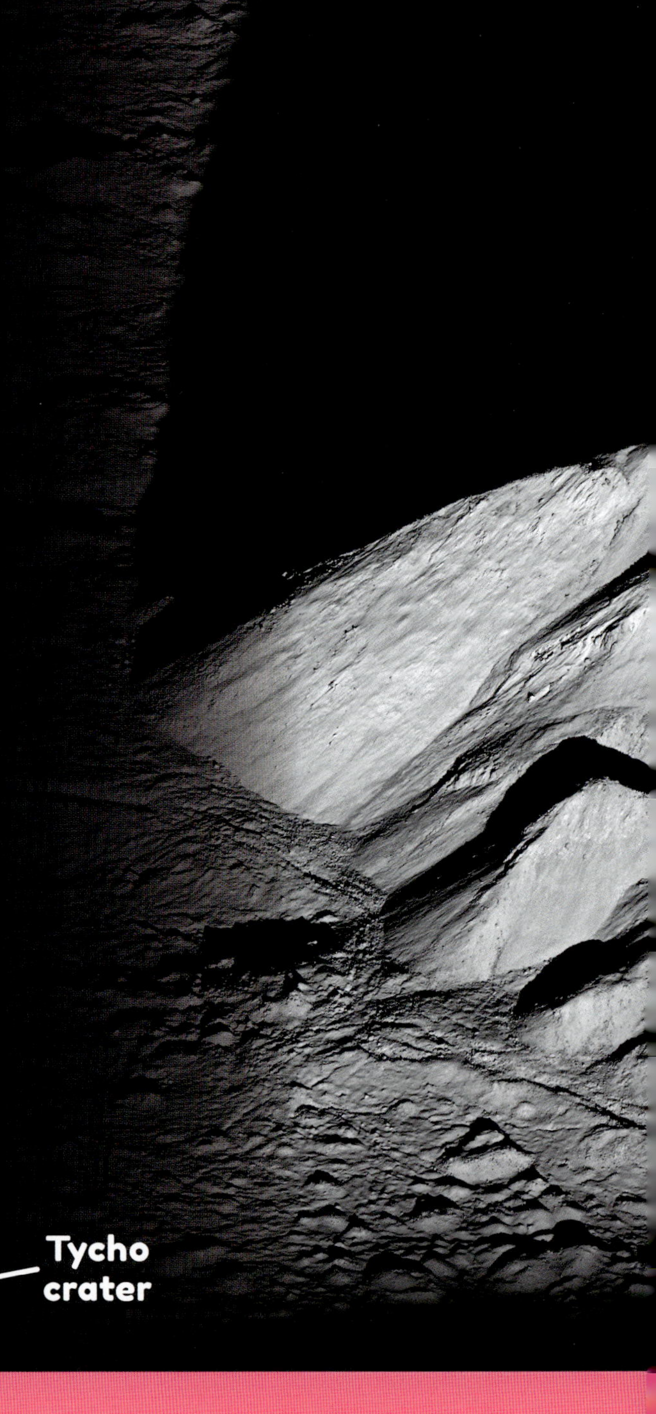

Tycho's
central peak

The twin GRAIL spacecraft worked together to study lunar gravity.

Gravity Recovery and Interior Laboratory (GRAIL)

The Gravity Recovery and Interior Laboratory (GRAIL) mission launched in September 2011. Its goal was to learn about the moon's gravity. GRAIL included two spacecraft. They were named *Ebb* and *Flow*.

Findings

Ebb and *Flow* both orbited the moon. Devices measured how their speeds changed over time. This allowed scientists to measure gravity's pull. Some areas of the moon have stronger gravity than others. GRAIL helped scientists map these differences.

Mascons

Some parts of the moon have stronger gravity than other parts. They are called mascons, or mass concentrations. Scientists believe that asteroid impacts created the mascons.

GRAIL's map shows areas of stronger gravity in red.

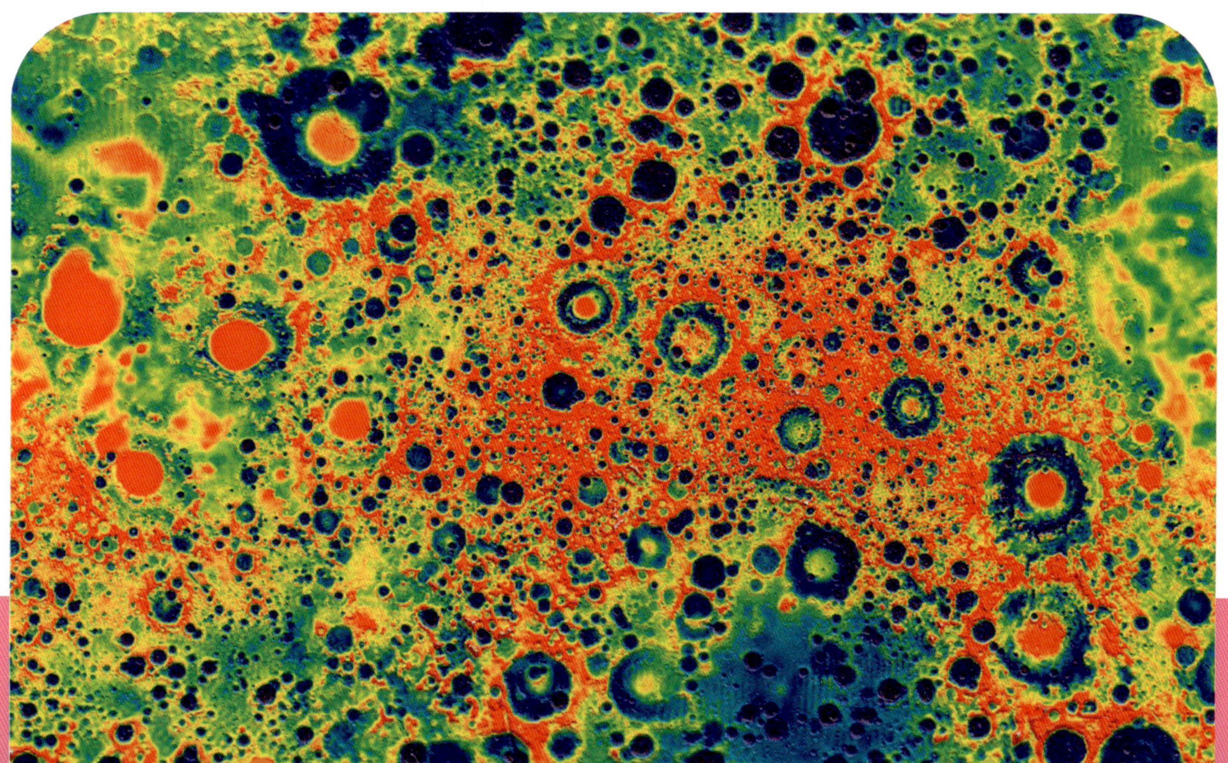

Lunar Atmosphere and Dust Environment Explorer (LADEE)

The *Lunar Atmosphere and Dust Environment Explorer* (*LADEE*) spacecraft launched in September 2013. It studied the moon's thin atmosphere. It measured the amount of dust in it. Scientists learned more about how this kind of atmosphere forms.

The *LADEE* spacecraft was covered in solar panels.

Exospheres

A thin atmosphere like the moon's is also called an exosphere. In the solar system, exospheres are common. Planets such as Mercury have them. So do moons such as Jupiter's Europa.

China's *Chang'e 3* lander brought a rover to the lunar surface.

Other Nations

The United States and the Soviet Union sent several landers to the moon first. But other nations have joined them. China landed the *Chang'e 3* spacecraft in 2013. India's *Chandrayaan-3* followed in 2023. And Japan's *Smart Lander for Investigating Moon* (*SLIM*) touched down in 2024.

SLIM

Japan's *SLIM* landed upside down. But it survived touchdown. It sent back useful data. It also sent out two small rovers.

Private Missions

NASA began the Commercial Lunar Payload Services (CLPS) program in 2018. Private companies could create their own lunar landers. NASA would help fund them. The company Intuitive Machines landed its Nova-C spacecraft in 2024. The company Firefly landed its Blue Ghost spacecraft in early 2025.

Firefly prepared Blue Ghost for launch at its headquarters in Texas.

Artemis Program

NASA is working on the Artemis program. This is the plan to return astronauts to the moon. The program will use the Space Launch System (SLS) rocket. Astronauts will launch in the Orion spacecraft. The Starship spacecraft will be used for landing. This vehicle is made by the company SpaceX.

The huge SLS rocket is an important part of the Artemis program.

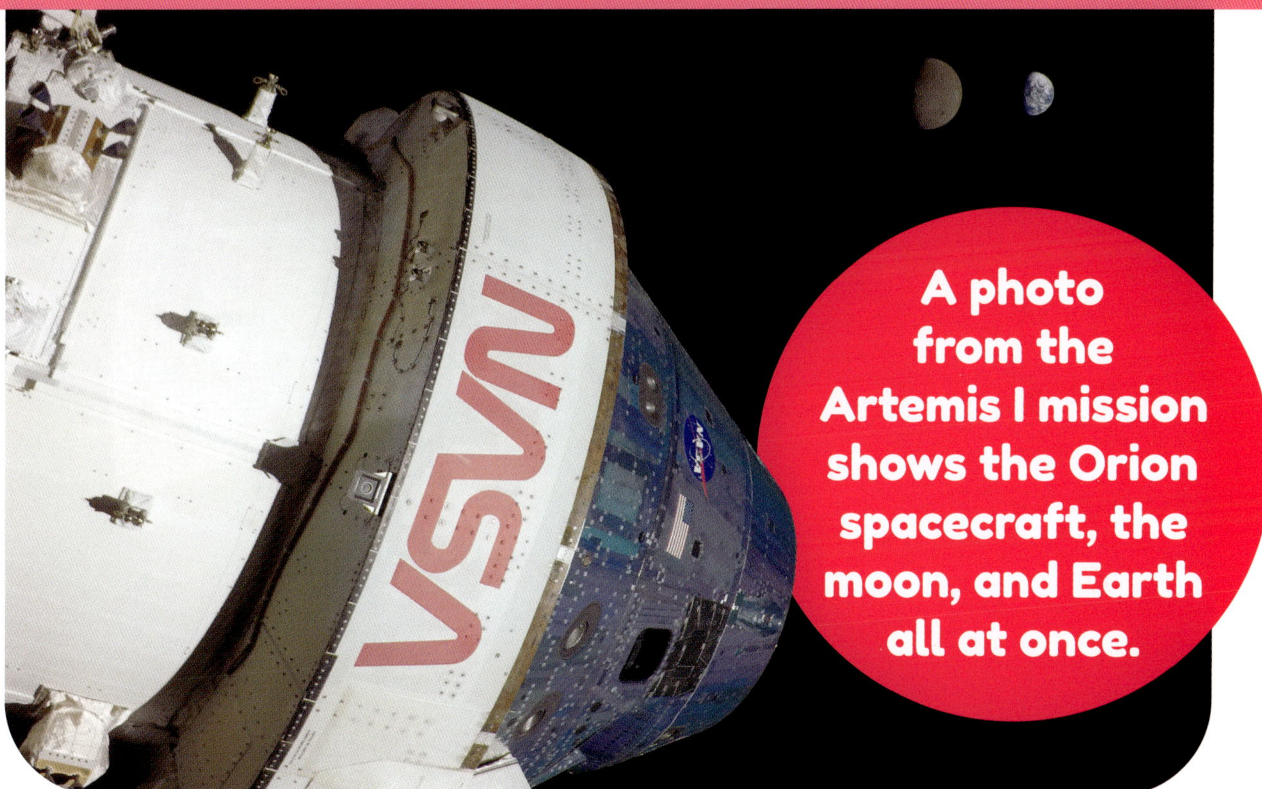

A photo from the Artemis I mission shows the Orion spacecraft, the moon, and Earth all at once.

Artemis I

The first Artemis mission launched in November 2022. Artemis I tested the SLS rocket and Orion spacecraft. It carried no crew. Orion orbited the moon. It successfully returned to Earth. NASA continued preparing for future human missions.

Back to the Moon

NASA planned for Artemis II to carry astronauts to lunar orbit. Artemis III was planned to be the program's first lunar landing.

The sun's gravity has kept the planets and moons in stable orbits for billions of years.

Gravity

Gravity is a force. It pulls objects with mass together. The more mass something has, the stronger its gravity. The sun's gravity holds the planets in orbit around the sun. Earth's gravity holds the moon in orbit around Earth.

The Moon's Orbit

The moon has much less mass than Earth. This means gravity is weaker there. On the moon's surface, gravity is six times weaker than on Earth. Objects weigh less than they do on Earth.

Moon Weight

A person who weighs 100 pounds (45 kg) on Earth would weigh just 17 pounds (7.7 kg) on the moon.

Astronaut John Young leaps while saluting the flag in the moon's low gravity.

Earth's Tilt

Earth rotates on its axis. This axis is not straight up and down. It tilts at an angle. This is called axial tilt. The moon's gravity helps keep this tilt stable. Without the moon, Earth might wobble more.

Earth's axis is tilted at 23.4 degrees.

The moon's axis is tilted at just 1.5 degrees.

Seasons

Earth's tilt means that sunlight does not hit the planet evenly. This causes the seasons. It is summer in places with direct sunlight. It is winter in places with less sunlight. The moon's axis has little tilt. This means the moon has no seasons.

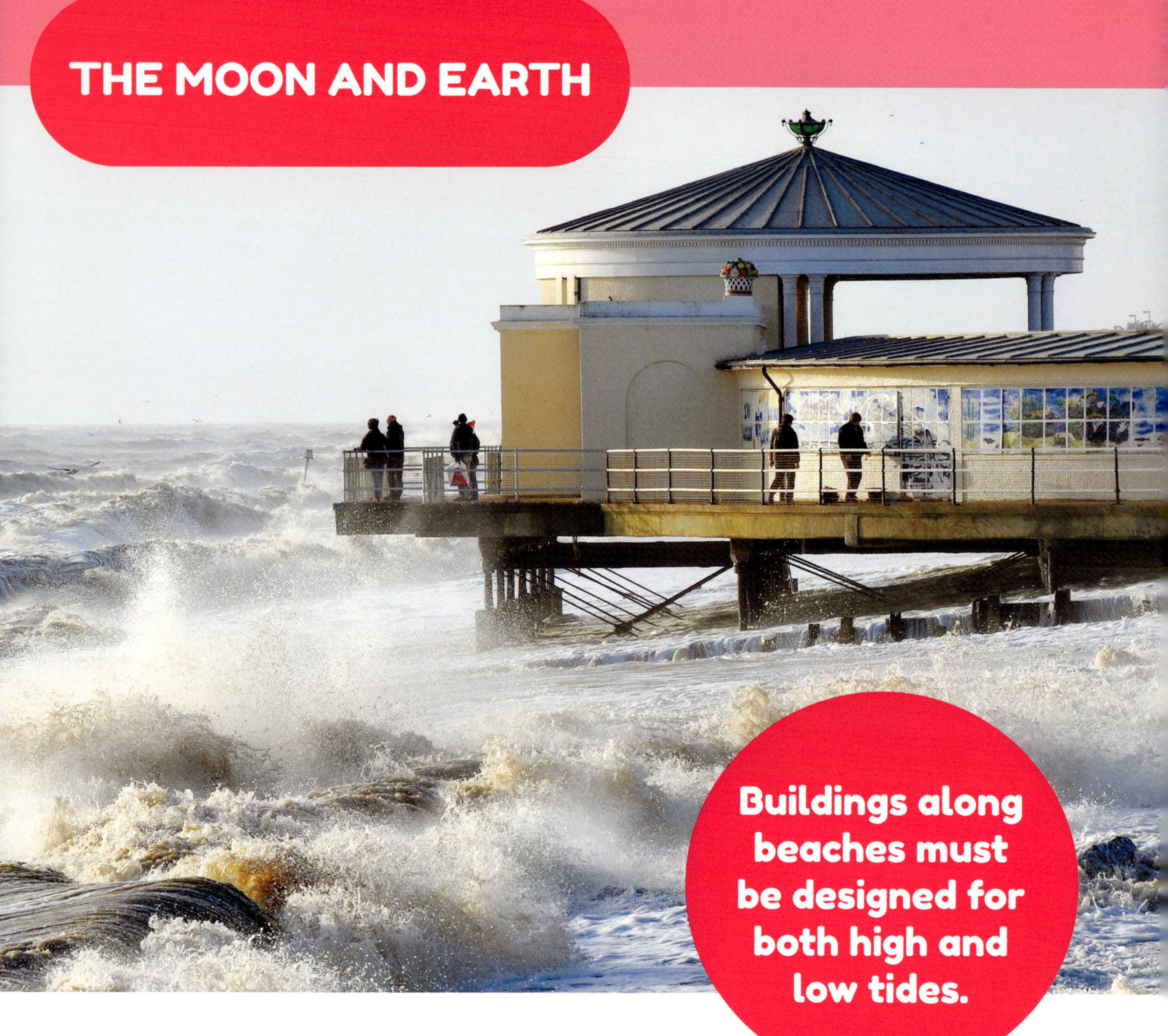

Buildings along beaches must be designed for both high and low tides.

What Are Tides?

Tides are the rise and fall of Earth's oceans. High tide happens when the water reaches its highest point on a beach. Its lowest point is low tide.

Pulling at the Oceans

The moon's gravity helps cause tides. It pulls at Earth's oceans. The parts of the ocean that are nearest to the moon bulge out. This area has high tide.

The moon and sun both affect Earth's tides.

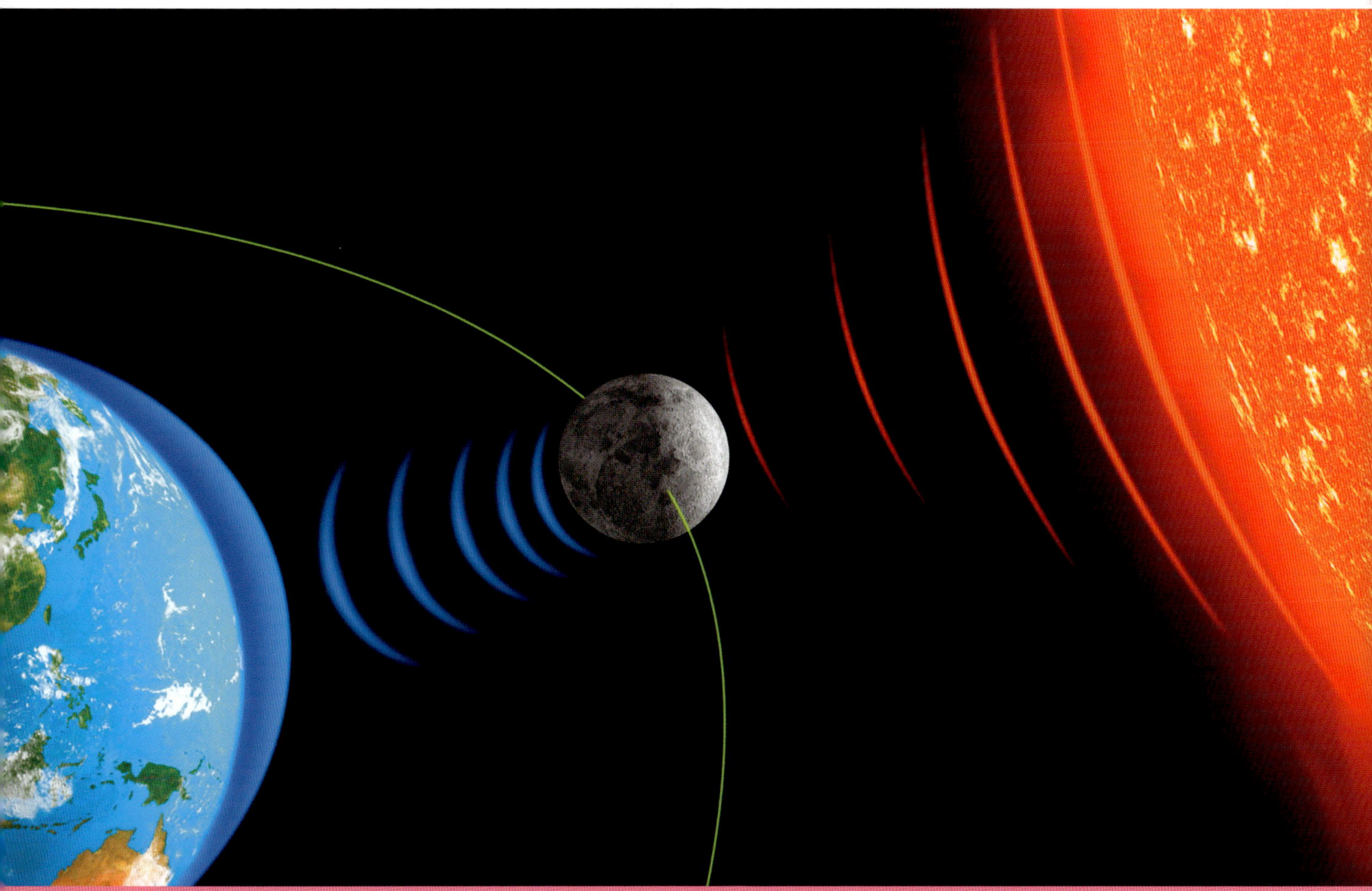

More Tides

Tides are not only in the oceans. This is just where they are easiest to see. Tides also occur in lakes. Tides happen in Earth's atmosphere. They are even in Earth's surface. The moon's gravity pulls at the whole planet.

Like the oceans, the atmosphere is affected by lunar gravity.

The Moon's Shape

The moon is shaped like a flattened ball. Scientists think Earth caused this. Long ago, Earth's gravity pulled the moon into this shape.

Tidally Locked

Earth and the moon are said to be tidally locked. People on Earth always see the same side of the moon. The moon is rotating as it orbits Earth. But one rotation takes the same time as one orbit.

Near Side and Far Side

The side facing Earth is called the near side. The other side is the far side. The two sides look different. The near side had more volcanoes in the past. This gives it a mix of light and dark areas. The far side has fewer dark features.

Humans first saw the far side of the moon in 1959, when a spacecraft took photos of it.

Far side

Solar Eclipse

Sometimes Earth, the sun, and the moon line up. The moon comes between Earth and the sun. The moon's shadow falls on Earth. This is a solar eclipse. To people on parts of Earth's surface, the sun is totally blocked. It becomes dark during the daytime. This lasts just a few minutes.

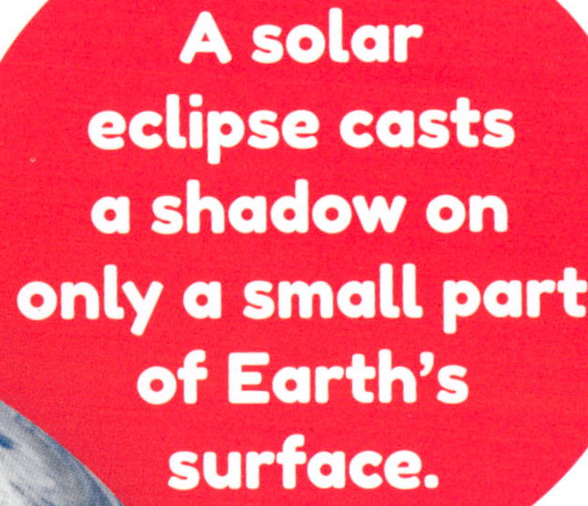

A lunar eclipse is visible anywhere on the half of Earth facing the moon.

Lunar Eclipse

Sometimes Earth comes between the sun and the moon. Earth's shadow falls on the moon. This is called a lunar eclipse. The moon takes on a dark red color. The color comes from light passing through Earth's atmosphere.

A full moon can be a dim source of light on a clear night.

Moonlight

People use the word *moonlight*. They say that the moon shines. But the moon doesn't give off light. It only reflects sunlight. At any time, half of the moon is lit. The other half is dark.

Phases

Sometimes the whole side of the moon facing Earth reflects sunlight. This is a full moon. Sometimes part of the lit side faces away from Earth. This is a crescent moon. When only the far side is lit up, the moon looks dark. This is called a new moon. Full, crescent, and new are some of the moon's phases.

The moon's appearance changes as it goes through its phases.

Lunar Samples

The six Apollo landings brought back 842 pounds (382 kg) of lunar samples. Three Soviet missions brought back 0.5 pounds (227 g). Two Chinese missions brought back 8.2 pounds (3.7 kg).

Geology

Geology is the study of rocks and landforms. Some scientists study lunar geology. This field looks at the moon's rocks and landforms. Scientists study rock samples. They also study photos of the moon's surface.

Samples from the Apollo program have taught scientists a lot about lunar geology.

Lunar Surface

Earth's outer layer is called the crust. It is made of rocky plates. These plates slowly move over time. They reshape the surface. The moon does not have moving rocky plates. Its outer surface does not change as Earth's does.

The moon took millions of years to cool after forming.

Lunar Magma Ocean

After the moon formed, it was hot and molten. The whole surface was one body of magma. Scientists call this the lunar magma ocean. It slowly cooled and hardened.

Differentiation

A process called differentiation happened to the early moon. It happened in the magma ocean. Heavy minerals sank. Lighter ones floated. These light minerals included plagioclase feldspar. This mineral formed the lunar surface. It became a rocky crust.

Today's lunar crust was made by differentiation in the moon's past.

Crust

The lunar crust is 38 to 63 miles (61 to 101 km) thick. It is covered with regolith. Regolith is lunar soil. It is thinnest in the maria. It is deepest in the highlands. It varies from 10 to 66 feet (3 to 20 m) thick.

The Apollo astronauts found that the moon has a thin layer of dust on top of the regolith.

Apollo 15 brought back a sample of dark basalt.

Crust Materials

The crust is mostly plagioclase feldspar. This mineral is rich in calcium. It makes up the light areas on the moon's surface. The dark areas were formed by volcanoes. They have a stone called basalt.

Mantle

The mantle is the layer beneath the crust. It extends down to the moon's core. The mantle is about 840 miles (1,350 km) thick. Like the crust, the mantle formed through differentiation.

Mantle Formation

Heavy minerals sank as they formed. One of these was ilmenite. It began near the mantle's top. The heavy ilmenite fell deeper into the mantle. It sank below lighter minerals.

Samples of ilmenite can be found on Earth.

Lava Flows

The ilmenite heated as it sank. It melted and became magma. The magma later returned to the surface. It hardened into rock. The Apollo astronauts found this rock. They brought samples back to Earth.

A microscopic photo of an Apollo 11 moon rock shows ilmenite in black.

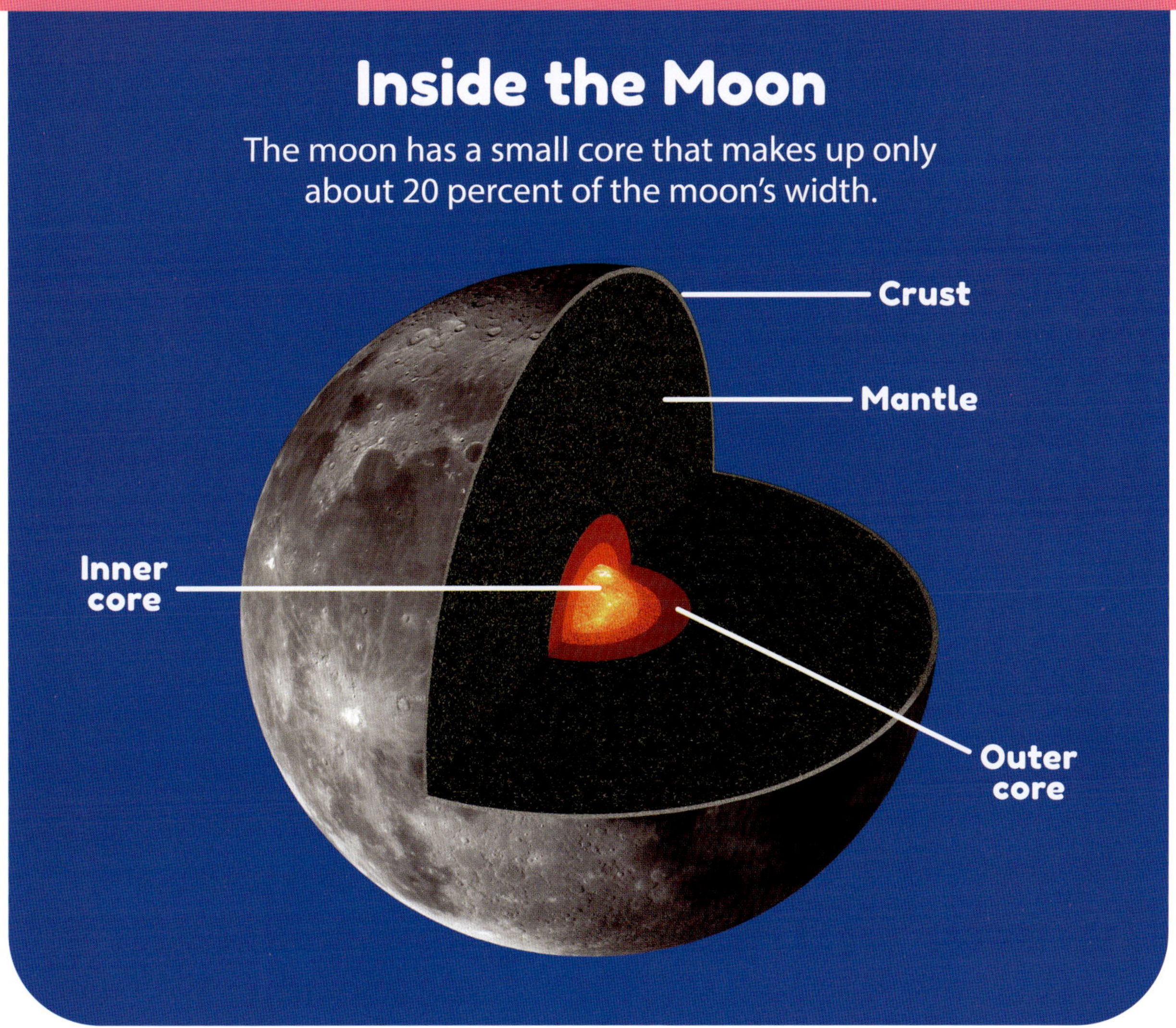

Core

At the moon's center is the core. The inner core is believed to be solid. It is rich in iron. It also has nickel. Scientists are still learning about the moon's core.

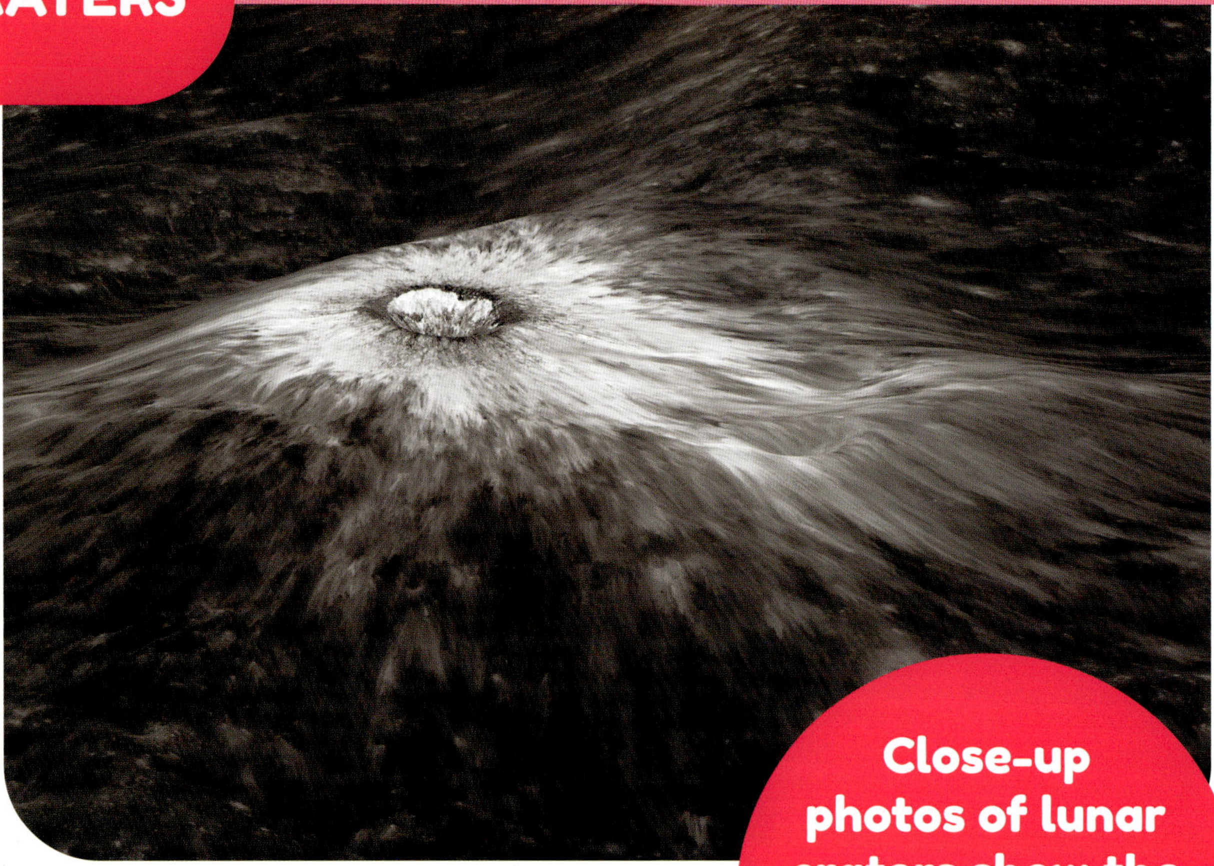

Close-up photos of lunar craters show the ejecta surrounding the point of impact.

Lunar Impacts

The moon is covered in many craters. These are impact craters. They form when something strikes the moon. Meteorites blast a dent into the surface. Rock and dust are thrown outward. These materials are called ejecta. Lines of ejecta can often be seen around craters.

Erosion

On Earth, wind wears away rock. So does water. This process is called erosion. Erosion wears away craters on Earth. The moon has no erosion. Craters can remain for millions of years.

Meteorite impacts stir the regolith. They bring underground material to the surface.

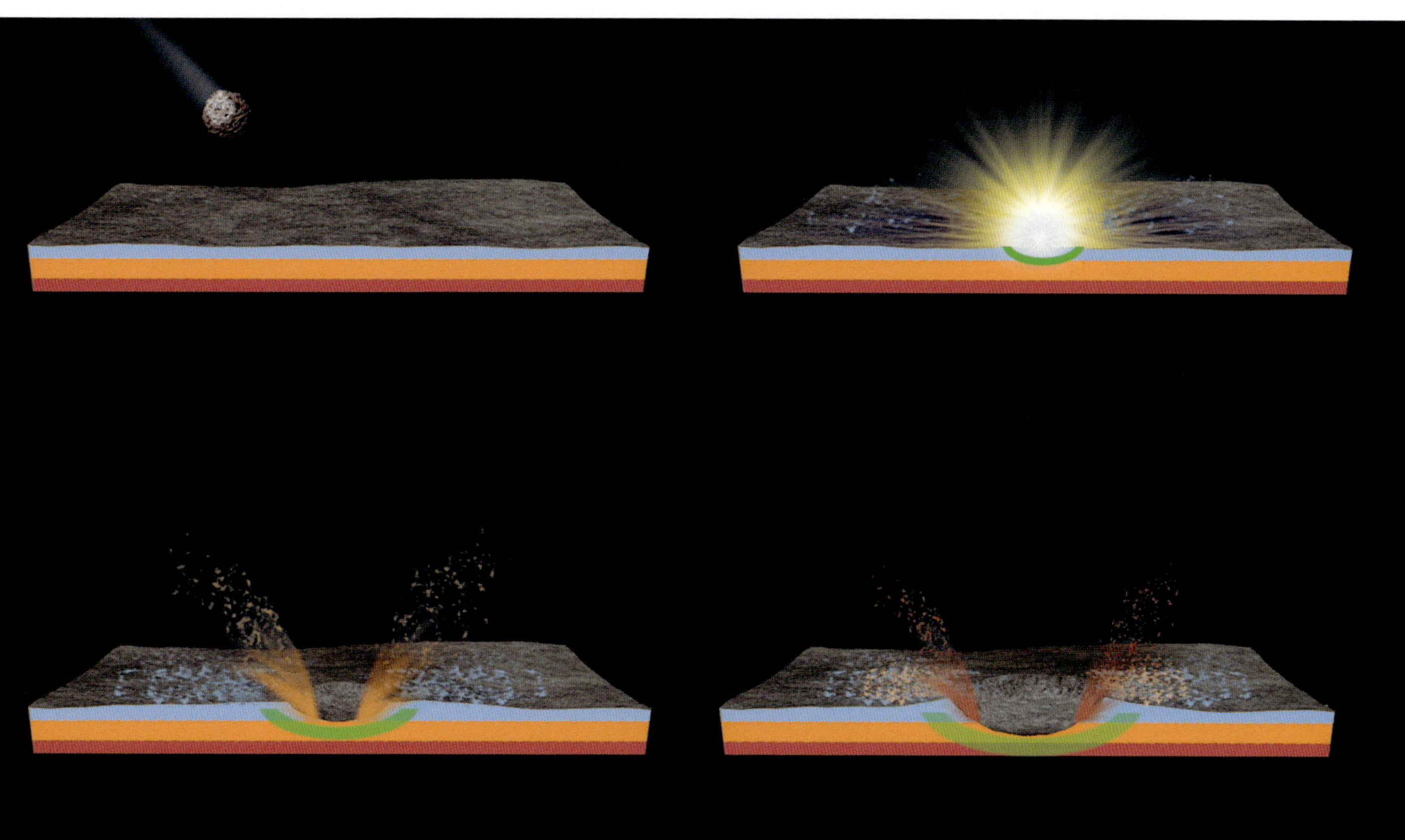

Simple Craters

There are three types of lunar craters. The first is a simple crater. It looks like an evenly round bowl. Small impacts cause these craters.

Simple craters are the smallest type.

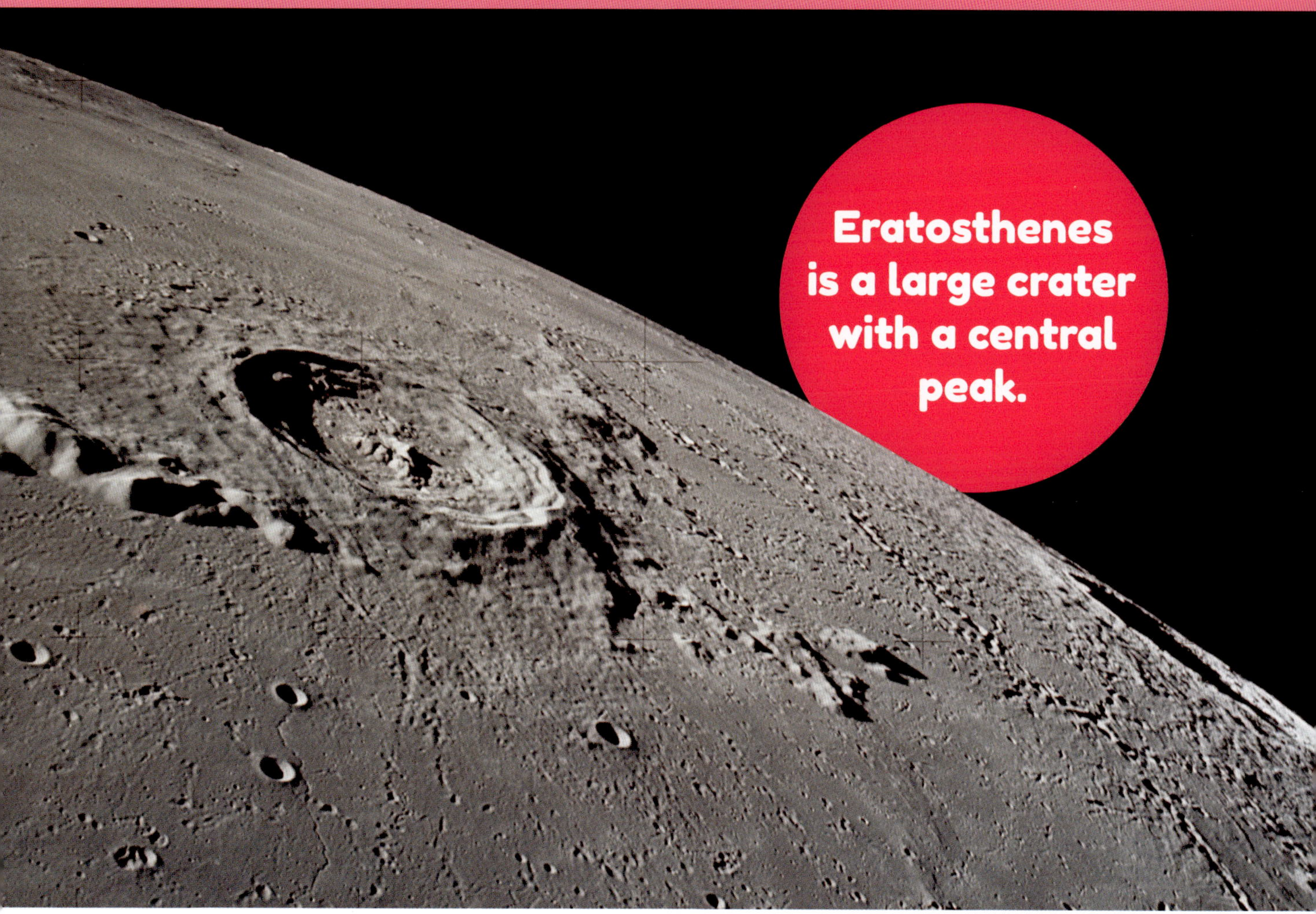

Complex Craters and Basins

Larger impacts create the second type. These are complex craters. They may have a peak in the center. Their edges are rough instead of smooth. Even bigger impacts create basins. These large, flat areas often have dark rock.

Impact gardening reshapes the moon's surface.

Impact Gardening

Meteorite impacts are powerful events. They throw ejecta upward. This ejecta hits the ground over a wide area. It stirs up material. It reveals fresh layers of regolith. This process is called impact gardening.

Dangers

Lunar impacts could be dangerous for human missions. A meteorite could strike a shelter. It could harm the structure. Air could leak out. Engineers must plan for these risks.

Future moon bases could be designed to protect against meteorites.

Highlands

The moon's highlands are light in color. They are made of a rock called anorthosite. This rock is mostly plagioclase feldspar. Mountains in the highlands are rounded and low. They aren't pointy like some Earth mountains.

The Apollo 16 astronauts explored the Descartes highlands.

Large and small craters dot the highland landscapes.

Old Areas

The highlands are the oldest areas on the moon. They have many craters. Some of these craters formed more than a billion years ago.

Apollo 11 landed in a mare called the Sea of Tranquility.

Maria

A dark area on the moon is called a mare. Together these areas are known as maria. These dark areas are low in elevation. The stone is different from highland stone.

Basalt

This darker stone is basalt. Basalt can be found on Earth. It is an igneous rock. This means it forms as lava cools. Basalt has iron and magnesium. These elements make the stone dark.

The maria are smoother, flatter, and darker than the highlands.

Creating Maria

When the moon was young, heat in the core melted rock. Magma rose up, and lava flowed from volcanoes. This lava filled many empty craters. It cooled and formed the flat, dark maria.

Both Earth and the moon were covered in lava in the time after their formation.

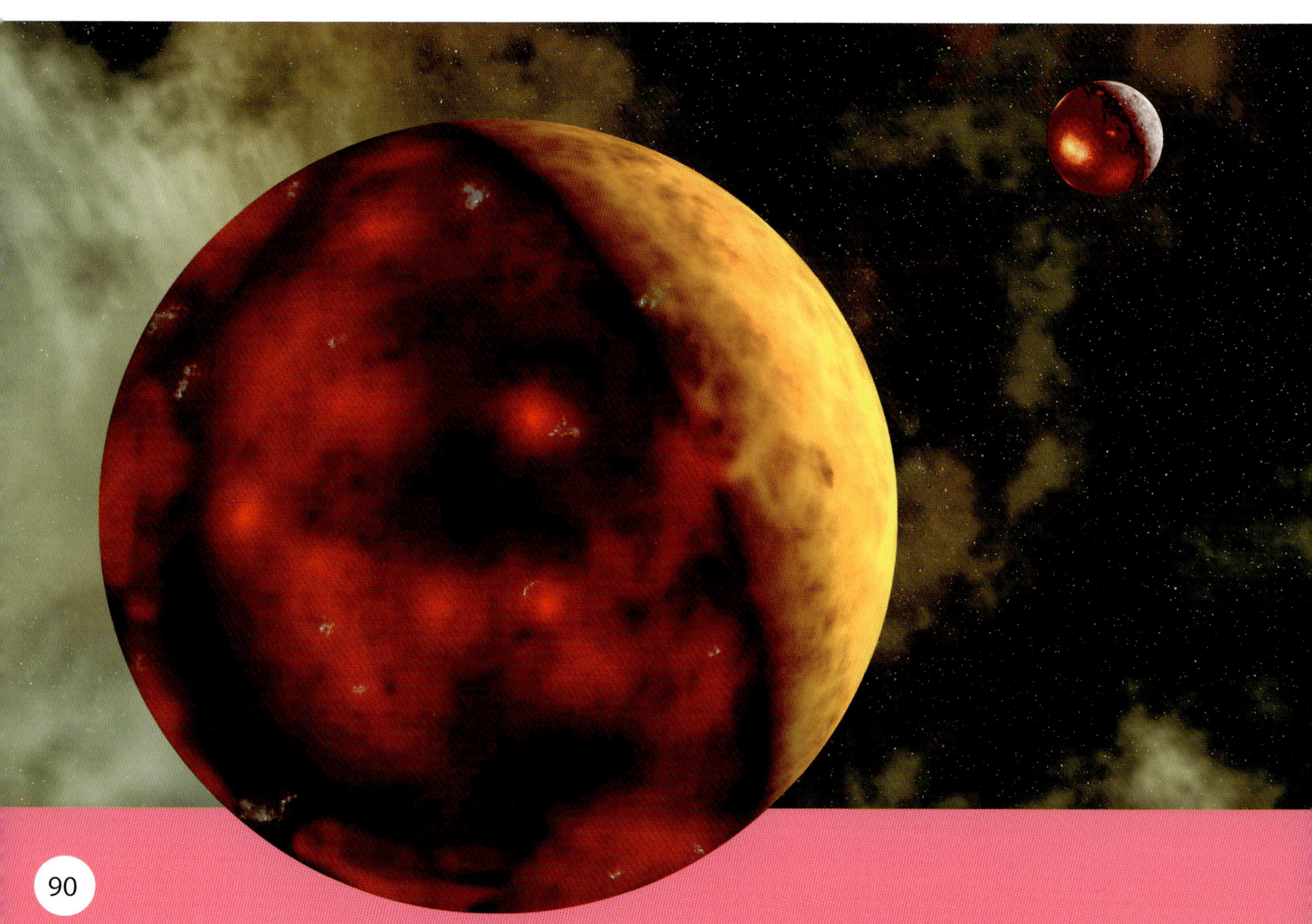

Astronauts collected soil samples from the Ocean of Storms.

Ocean of Storms

The largest mare is called Oceanus Procellarum. This name means "Ocean of Storms." It is 1,600 miles (2,575 km) across.

FUN FACT!

The Apollo 12 mission landed in the Ocean of Storms.

An image from *LRO* shows the Ocean of Storms.

Forming the Ocean

Scientists once thought an impact created the Ocean of Storms. Smaller basins formed this way. But the GRAIL mission provided new evidence.

GRAIL Discoveries

GRAIL measured gravity in the Ocean of Storms. Differences in gravity showed the locations of underground lava tubes. Scientists think lava from these tubes formed the Ocean of Storms.

GRAIL revealed new data about the Ocean of Storms.

KREEP

Scientists noticed a pattern in lunar rocks. The rocks have a mix of elements. One is potassium. Its chemical symbol is K. They also have rare earth elements (REE). Finally, they have phosphorus. Its symbol is P. Scientists call this combination KREEP.

Astronauts used a rake-like tool to gather rock samples.

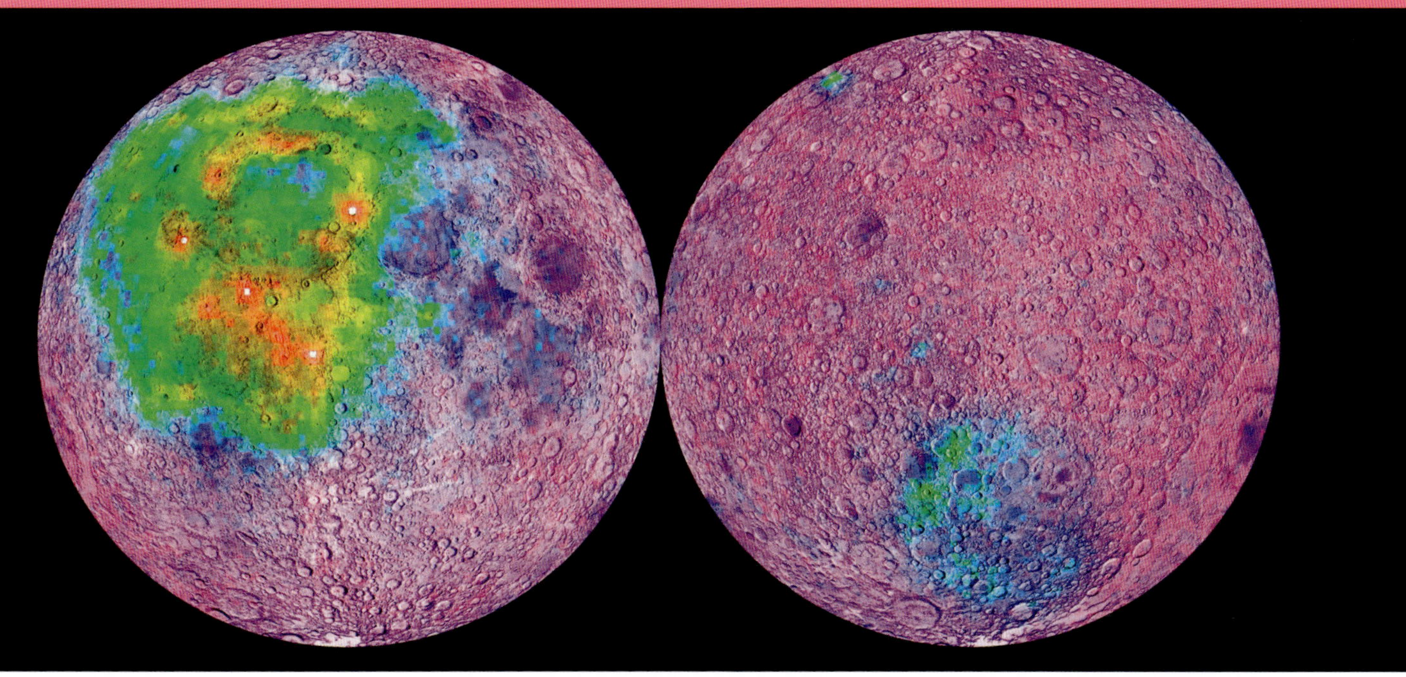

This NASA map shows the locations where thorium is found. Green, yellow, and red show more of this element. It occurs in places with KREEP rocks.

Locating KREEP

Every Apollo mission brought back KREEP rocks. This led scientists to think the rocks were common everywhere on the moon. But later studies found surprising results. Most of the moon does not have KREEP rocks. The landings just happened to be in places where they are common.

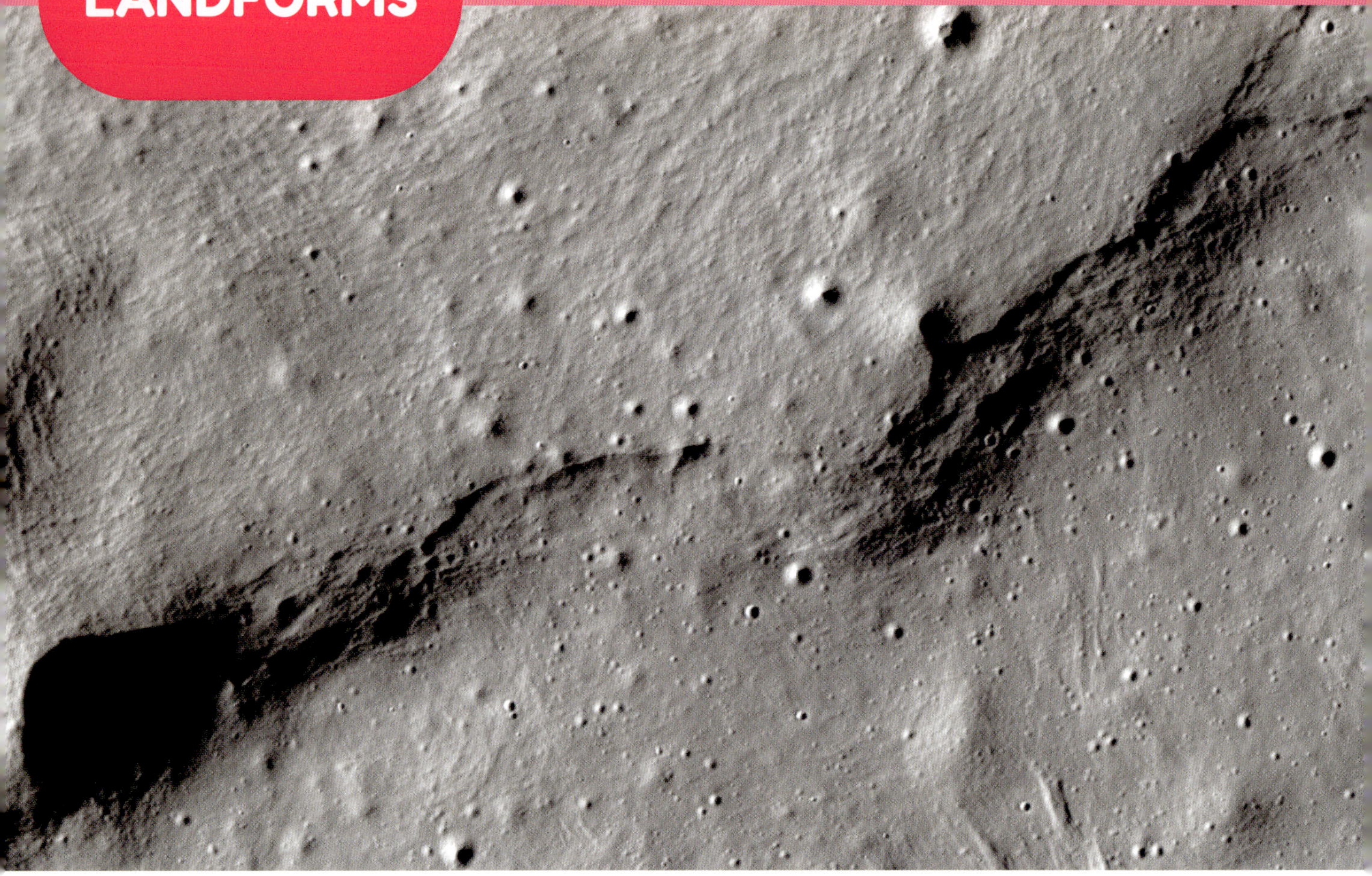

LRO took images of lobate scarps.

Lobate Scarps

The moon has lobate scarps. These look like long cliffs. They rise steeply on one side and have a gentle slope on the other.

FUN FACT!

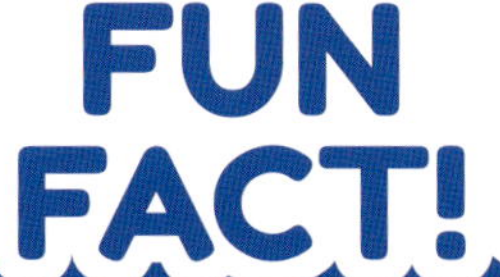

The Apollo 17 astronauts drove their lunar rover along a scarp.

Forming Scarps

The moon still has heat from its formation. As the moon cools, it shrinks slightly. This causes the crust to snap. It forms a lobate scarp.

An illustration of the Apollo 17 landing site shows a scarp.

Scarp

Jerry Elmore

Silicic Domes

The moon has structures called silicic domes. These are bright hills. They rise above the dark basalt around them.

An image from *LRO* shows silicic domes in the Ocean of Storms.

An area called the Marius Hills has many small domes.

Questions Remain

The rock in these domes has a lot of silica. It has little iron oxide. The result is a bright color. Silicic domes form from silica magma. This is different from the magma that creates basalt. Scientists are still figuring out how silicic domes formed.

The moon's atmosphere is so thin that distant objects do not appear blurry. This can make it tough to tell how far away something is.

Atmosphere

The moon has a very thin atmosphere. It has several elements. These include helium, neon, argon, and others. Scientists do not know where these gases come from.

Temperature

Earth's thick atmosphere keeps temperatures stable. But the moon's atmosphere is too thin to do this. Temperatures vary a lot. Daytime temperatures reach 273 degrees Fahrenheit (134°C). At night, it gets as cold as –243 degrees Fahrenheit (–153°C).

Space suits keep astronauts comfortable as they move between sun and shade.

Lunar Desert

Scientists once thought the moon had no water. Without an atmosphere, any water would quickly dry up. The moon was seen as a huge desert.

Armstrong compared the appearance of the lunar landscape to deserts in the United States.

Scientists combined many images from *Clementine* for this view of the moon's north pole.

Water on the Moon?

These ideas changed over time. Scientists wondered if the moon's craters might have water. It would be in the form of ice. The *Clementine* spacecraft found evidence for this. But scientists were not totally sure.

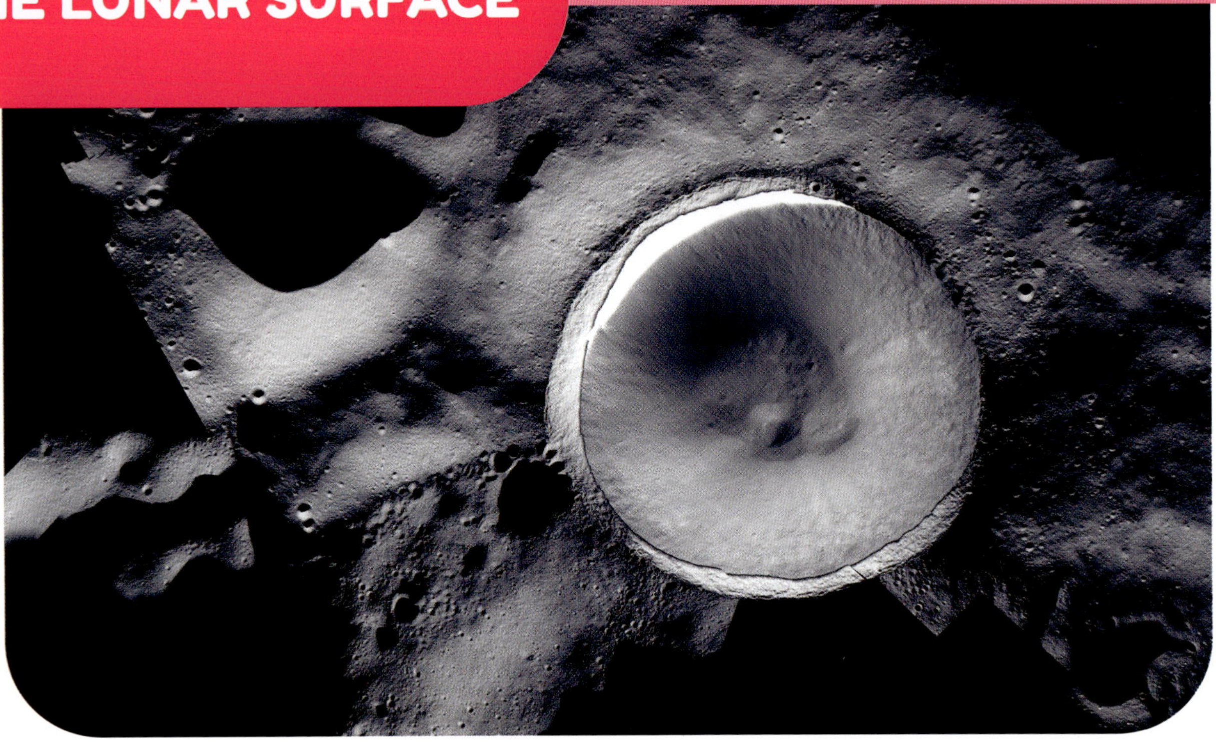

The large crater Shackleton is located at the moon's south pole.

Ice in Craters

Later missions supported this idea. In 2018, a spacecraft found ice in craters near the moon's poles. The bottoms of these craters never get sunlight. They are always in shadow.

NASA created a special camera called ShadowCam. It is designed to get clear views of dark craters.

Water on the Surface

Scientists later discovered water in sunlit areas. A NASA telescope studied the crater Clavius in 2020. It found water on the surface. In 35 cubic feet (1 cubic m) of soil, there are about 12 ounces (350 mL) of water.

The 2020 study of Clavius was done by a flying NASA observatory called SOFIA.

Solar Wind

Solar wind is a stream of particles from the sun. The particles are electrons and protons. They flow out into the solar system.

Particles are constantly streaming away from the sun.

Astronauts set up sheet-like devices to take samples of the solar wind.

Hitting the Moon

Earth has a magnetic field. It blocks the solar wind, protecting life on the planet. But the moon has no magnetic field. The solar wind strikes the moon. It creates static electricity.

Lava caves on the moon could provide shelter from CMEs.

Coronal Mass Ejections (CMEs)

Sometimes there are giant eruptions on the sun. Material and energy blast out of the surface. This is called a coronal mass ejection (CME).

Harmful Energy

CMEs send high-energy particles to the moon. In 2021, scientists measured a CME that reached the moon. They found that its energy could harm astronauts. Future astronauts may have to find shelter during CMEs.

Coronal mass ejections are striking events.

Dust on Earth

On Earth, dust is made of tiny pieces of soil. Erosion wears away the sharp edges of these pieces. Dust may be annoying. But it is usually not dangerous.

Driving on dirt roads can kick up dust on Earth.

The Apollo 17 astronauts had to repair their rover's wheel cover. It had broken off, and the rover was throwing up too much dust.

Moon Dust

On the moon, dust is made of crushed rock. Erosion does not smooth its edges. Moon dust is sharp. This can create serious problems for human missions.

The Apollo astronauts' white suits became coated with dust.

Dust Danger

Moon dust has an electrical charge. It clings to space suits. The sharp pieces can harm the suits. When astronauts return to their spacecraft, they carry dust with them. Breathing it in can harm the lungs.

Apollo astronauts reported that moon dust smells like burnt gunpowder.

Solutions

Moon dust cannot be brushed off. NASA is making a dusting device instead. It is easy to use. The handheld duster does not blow air. Instead, it changes the dust's charge. The dust stops sticking to objects.

NASA scientists tested a new anti-dust device in 2018.

Moonquakes

The moon is still cooling. As it cools, it shrinks. This leads to moonquakes. The quakes are near the surface of the moon. Cracks or fault lines can appear. The Apollo missions recorded shallow moonquakes.

Apollo astronauts set up devices to detect shaking in the ground.

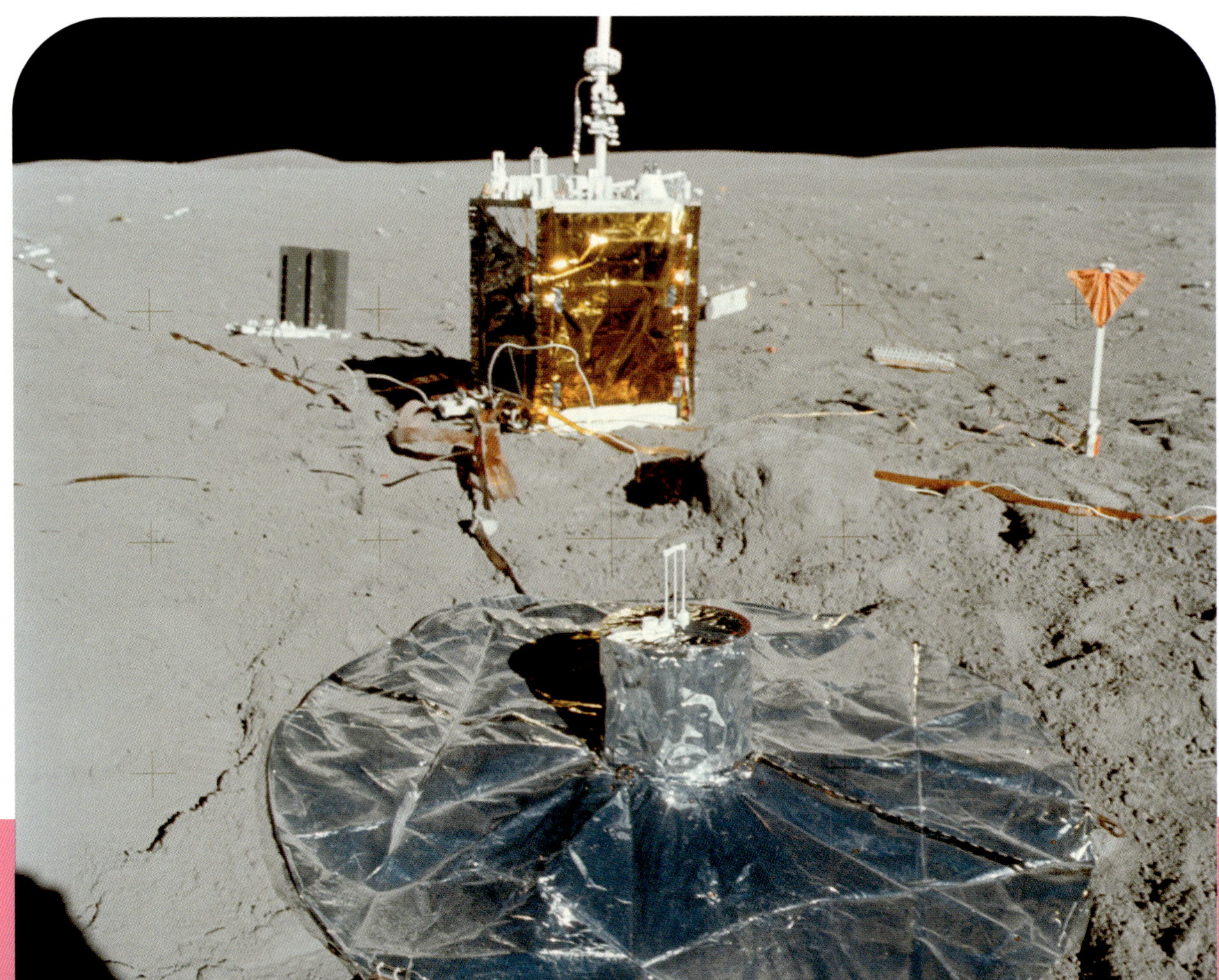

Fault Lines

Some fault lines are found near the moon's south pole. Future human missions will land in this area. Astronauts will look for ice there. Moonquakes could be dangerous for these missions.

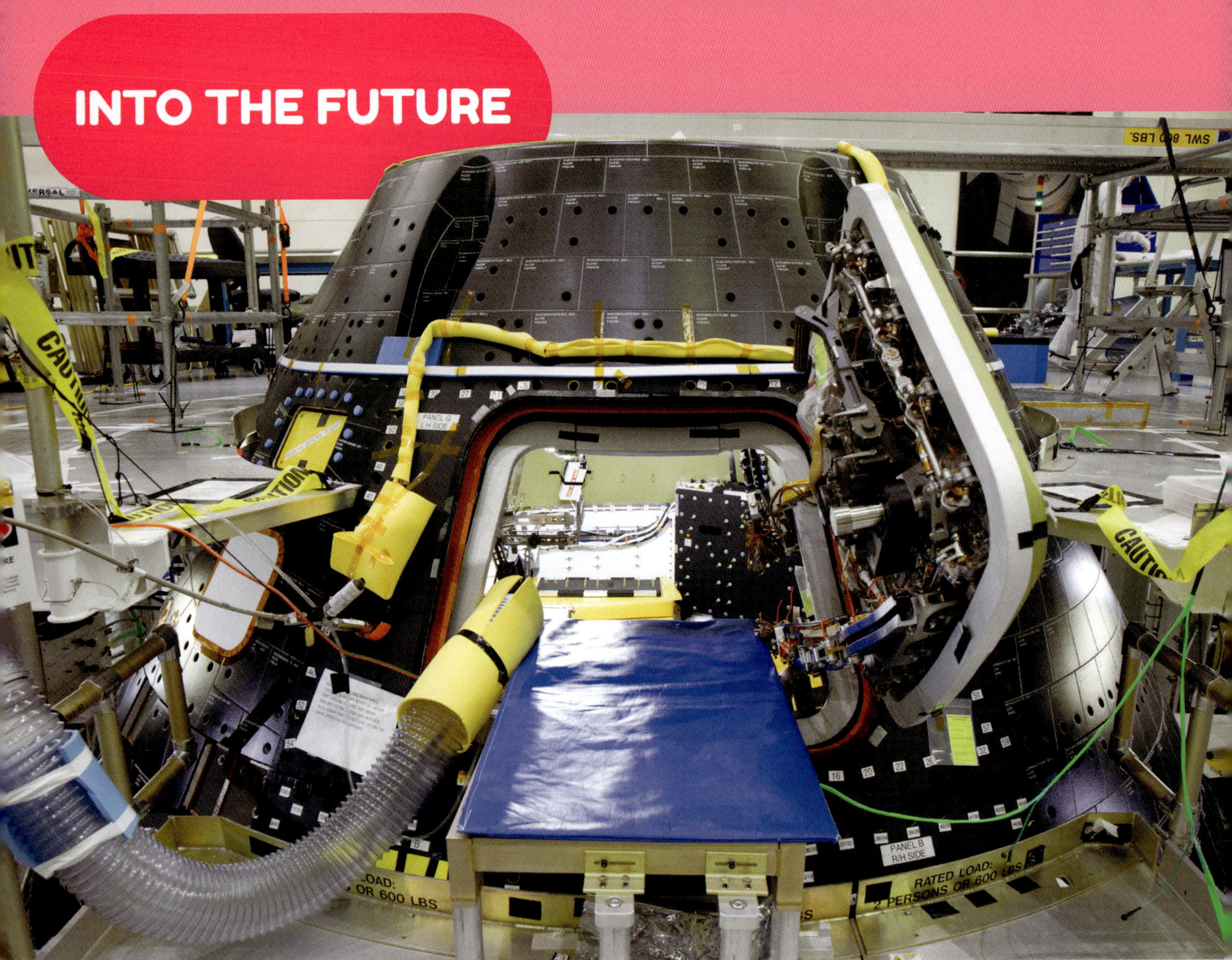

NASA worked on new spacecraft for the Artemis program in the early 2020s.

Moon Base

The Artemis program will send people back to the moon. They will live and work there. They will test things needed for future missions to Mars.

Working Together

NASA is leading the Artemis program. But the program also includes other nations. These nations will help work on spacecraft. Their astronauts will join landings on the moon.

Canadian astronaut Jeremy Hansen trained for Artemis missions.

Lunar Gateway

NASA is planning a new space station called Lunar Gateway. It will orbit the moon. Astronauts will visit it during Artemis missions. They will stop there before landing.

Space Science

Lunar Gateway will also be a laboratory. Scientists will study human health, biology, and physics. This work will be helpful for future missions.

An illustration shows a spacecraft, *left*, approaching Lunar Gateway.

Workers built the parts of Lunar Gateway in the mid-2020s.

Assembly in Space

Lunar Gateway is too large to launch in one piece. Instead, the pieces will be launched separately. Astronauts will connect the pieces together. The station will grow larger over time.

Future astronauts may explore the moon's surface for ice.

South Pole

NASA has plans for a base at the moon's south pole. Ice is believed to be in this area of the moon. Astronauts will stay at the base for one to two months.

Low Gravity

The moon's low gravity will be a challenge. Living in low gravity for a long time weakens bones and muscles. It can affect the eyes. NASA will study how to keep astronauts healthy.

Astronauts living in orbit must exercise often. The same may be true of astronauts on the moon.

Transportation

NASA will need to send equipment and supplies to the moon. Powerful rockets are being designed to do this. New rovers will let astronauts travel on the surface.

In 2024, the Japanese space agency signed an agreement to create a new rover for the Artemis program.

Energy

The moon base will need dependable energy. Some may come from solar panels. These turn sunlight into electricity. The base might also use small nuclear reactors. These will be like tiny forms of the nuclear power plants on Earth.

Future spacecraft could launch from the moon after refueling there.

Water to Fuel

Water on the moon could be turned into rocket fuel. Water can be split into oxygen and hydrogen. These elements can fuel rockets. Making fuel on the moon will make more exploration possible.

Finding Useful Materials

Astronauts will use rovers to explore the moon's surface. They will search for water and other natural materials. Practicing this on the moon will help astronauts prepare for future missions. Someday people may travel to Mars and beyond.

The next generation of lunar explorers will add to our knowledge of the moon.

GLOSSARY

agency
A part of a government that does a particular job.

atmosphere
The gases that surround an object in space.

axis
An invisible line that runs up and down through a moon or planet's middle and that it spins around.

basalt
A dark volcanic rock.

designed
Built to do something.

elevation
How high something is.

evidence
Information that helps support an idea.

focus
How lenses change the direction of rays of light.

material
Matter.

mineral
A solid, natural material.

mission
A task or job.

module
A major part of a larger spacecraft.

molten
Heated into a liquid form.

orbit
To follow a curved path around another object.

particle
A tiny piece of something.

probe
A remotely controlled device that explores space.

theory
A scientific guess based on evidence.

TO LEARN MORE

More Books to Read

Hirsch, Andy. *Human Spaceflight: Rockets and Rivalry*. First Second, 2023.

Huddleston, Emma. *Explore the Moon*. Abdo, 2022.

Ringstad, Arnold. *Astronauts*. Abdo, 2026.

Online Resources

To learn more about the moon, please visit **abdobooklinks.com** or scan this QR code. These links are routinely monitored and updated to provide the most current information available.

PHOTO CREDITS

Cover Photos: Paitoon Pornsuksomboon/Shutterstock Images, front; Adobe Stock, back

Interior Photos: Shutterstock Images, 1, 3, 4 (top), 4 (bottom), 5, 8, 12, 14 (bottom), 36 (top), 38 (bottom), 41 (bottom), 46, 49 (top), 52 (bottom), 55 (bottom), 57 (top), 62, 63, 68, 70 (top), 76, 85, 106, 110, 118 (top); Flickr, 6; Diego Barucco/Shutterstock Images, 7; Ron Miller/Science Source, 9; Jacques Dayan/Shutterstock Images, 10, 61; James Blair/NASA, 11; Universal History Archive/Universal Images Group/Getty Images, 13, 18; DEA/ICAS94/De Agostini/Getty Images, 14 (top); Science & Society Picture Library/Getty Images, 15; Lukasz Pawel Szczepanski/Shutterstock Images, 16; Library of Congress/Science Source, 17; Keystone-France/Gamma-Keystone/Getty Images, 19; Bettmann/Getty Images, 20, 23; Detlev van Ravenswaay/Science Source, 21, 26, 27; Ria Novosti/AFP/Getty Images, 22; NASA, 24, 28, 30, 32, 36 (bottom), 38 (top), 39, 42, 43, 44, 45, 46–47, 48, 49 (bottom), 50, 51, 55 (top), 59, 66, 70 (bottom), 73, 75, 78, 80, 82, 83, 84, 87, 89, 91, 92, 93, 95, 96, 97, 98, 99, 100, 103, 104, 108, 111, 112, 114, 118 (bottom), 121, 125; NASA/JPL/Science Source, 25; Smithsonian, 29; Rolls Press/Popperfoto/Getty Images, 31; Harrison H. Schmitt/NASA, 33, 40, 41 (top); Bill Anders/NASA, 34; Russell L. Schweickart/NASA, 35; Neil A. Armstrong/NASA, 37, 88, 101, 107; Xinhua News Agency/Getty Images, 52 (top); Raquel Natalicchio/Houston Chronicle/Hearst Newspapers/Getty Images, 53; Jason Parrish/NASA, 54; Vadim Sadovski/Shutterstock Images, 56; Charles M. Duke Jr./NASA, 57 (bottom), 86; Carlos Clarivan/Science Source, 58; Barry Goble/Shutterstock Images, 60; Mark Garlick/Science Source, 64, 65; Chris Harwood/Shutterstock Images, 67; Somchai Som/Shutterstock Images, 69; Eugene A. Cernan/NASA, 71; David A. Hardy/Science Source, 72, 124; Buzz Aldrin/NASA, 74; Susan E. Degginger/Science Source, 77; Gregoire Cirade/Science Source, 79, 120; Tim Brown/Science Source, 81; Walter Myers/Science Source, 90; Eugene Cernan/NASA, 94; Edwin E. Aldrin Jr./NASA, 102; Jim Ross/NASA, 105; NASA/GSFC/Arizona State University/Science Source, 109; Kim Shiflett/NASA, 113, 116; ESA/Foster + Partners/Science Source, 115; Robert Markowitz/NASA, 117; Josh Valcarcel/NASA, 119; Bill Ingalls/NASA, 122; P. Carril/European Space Agency/Science Source, 123